Fishy's Favorites

for Bass, Trout, and Salt Water

D1616683

Fishy's Favorites

for Bass, Trout, and Salt Water

Jay "Fishy" Fullum

STACKPOLE
BOOKS

Published by
STACKPOLE BOOKS
5067 Ritter Road
Mechanicsburg, PA 17055
www.stackpolebooks.com

Printed in the United States

10 9 8 7 6 5 4 3 2 1

First edition

Cover drawings by Jay "Fishy" Fullum
Cover design by Caroline Stover

Library of Congress Cataloging-in-Publication Data

Fullum, Jay.
    Fishy's favorites for bass, trout, and salt water / Jay Fullum.
        p.   cm.
    ISBN-13: 978-0-8117-3252-9
    ISBN-10: 0-8117-3252-5
    1. Fly tying.   2. Flies, Artificial.   3. Bass fishing.
4. Trout fishing.   5. Saltwater fishing.   I. Title.
SH451.F858   2006
688.7'9124–dc22

                                        2005015038

Contents

Foreword

Learning to tie flies is an evolutionary process. While swimming in the fly-tying primordial ooze, a prospective tier learns to start the thread on the hook and fashion a rudimentary fly. This initial attempt will look rough, and it might or might not catch a fish, but it is the first rung on the ladder to becoming a fly tier.

The next step in fly tying is to create a few well-recognized patterns—the Woolly Bugger and Hare's Ear Nymph fall somewhere in this early stage of development. If he sticks with it, a tier will learn to dress more complicated patterns: Catskill dry flies, Atlantic salmon flies, and maybe epoxy-headed saltwater patterns. He will get bitten by the fly-tying bug, buy more materials, and tie yet more flies. Over the years, he will mature from being a novice to becoming an apprentice and eventually a journeyman.

While there's a sense of accomplishment in becoming a proficient fly tier, I think a novice has more fun. An expert can become hidebound and set in his ways; a beginner doesn't know the traditional parameters that define what constitutes a "proper" fly, and so experiments and concocts all sorts of zany patterns. Just like a child, the novice doesn't know the rules, and so everything is fair game.

Jay "Fishy" Fullum is a very proficient fly tier, but he hasn't become stifled by tradition or lost his sense of imagination. He is always on the lookout for new materials, and is constantly cooking up fresh patterns. In a craft that can get stuffy with tradition, Fishy is a welcome breath of fresh air.

In addition to being a talented fly tier and accomplished angler, Fishy is also a patient teacher and mentor to thousands of other tiers and fishermen. I've seen him at dozens of fly-fishing shows where he always seems to be in the middle of a crowd of people, and everyone is laughing and having a good time. I once said it in the pages of *Fly Tyer* magazine: Jay Fullum is a goodwill ambassador for fly fishing.

Okay, enough about Fishy. You get the point: I think very highly of him, as well as his lovely wife, Carol. They're first-rate people. But what about his flies—will they really catch fish, or are they just gimmicks made from scraps found in the sales bin at the local craft store?

Over the years, I've test driven many of his original trout patterns around some of our best rivers. I've cast his warmwater flies to bass and panfish. I have also experimented with Jay's saltwater creations. I can truthfully say that his flies do indeed catch fish—a lot of them. And more than that, they're a hoot to tie.

Thumb through the pages of this book. Can you honestly say that you would not enjoy tying many of the patterns featured in this volume? I know they'll put a smile on your face when you see them sitting in the vise, and they will really make you grin when they catch fish. But more than the finished patterns, this collection of unique flies teaches lessons about creativity and the use of materials. Fishy demonstrates that there are no limits to how we tie or the materials we use: think creatively, think expansively, and have fun.

Along with being an expert angler, inventive tier, and thoughtful teacher, Fishy is a multitalented artist. He works in many mediums, but most of us know him for his instructional watercolors, the kind you'll find in the pages of this book. I once read the results of a poll taken of *Fly Tyer* magazine readers. One of the questions asked, "Who is your favorite author?" Our readers nominated a lot of great angling writers, and Fishy garnered dozens of well-deserved votes. Several readers specifically mentioned his talents as an artist, and a couple even said he should illustrate the articles written by other contributors. That's high praise from a group of discerning readers.

Jay "Fishy" Fullum is keeping the fun and creativity in fly tying. So, wherever you are on the fly-tying evolutionary ladder, read this book, tie the flies, and enjoy.

David Klausmeyer
Editor, *Fly Tyer* magazine

Introduction

I began tying flies soon after receiving a fly-tying kit as a present on December 25, 1951. My first fifteen years at the vise were a wonderful learning experience. I tied thousands of established patterns for everything from panfish to stream trout. My time at the vise had made me a better tier, and I was soon receiving small orders for my flies. The number of orders and the quantity of flies increased, and by the end of the next fishing season I had earned enough to purchase my first "good" fly rod.

Shortly after the holidays, I received a phone call from one of the local fly shops. The store tier had decided to move south, and they were interested in seeing a few samples of my flies. Twenty years later, I had commercially tied a zillion dozen flies for fly shops in three northeastern states. I made a few dollars at the vise, but my fingers were getting very short, as was my love for fly tying. An order for a hundred dozen Muddler Minnows finally ended my commercial tying career. By the time I completed the orders that spring, I didn't want to look at another hook clamped in the jaws of my vise.

It was sometime in late June when I ran out of one of my favorite patterns. I was tempted to pay the retail price for the drys–the same flies for which I had been paid the wholesale price shortly before the season opened. Reluctantly, I decided to sit down at the vise for the first time in several months. I was a bit rusty, but I quickly replenished my supply of drys.

As I sat there looking at the last fly still clamped in the jaws of the vise, my thoughts returned to a time when I truly loved to tie flies. Then and there I decided that my remaining years at the vise were going to be *fun*. Since then, I have enjoyed every moment spent at the vise. I hope that the fun I have at my vise is passed on to you as you tie your way through *Fishy's Favorites*.

Acknowledgments

A special thanks to my wife, Carol, who supports my efforts and makes the many hours we share on the water a joy. I thank my daughter, Lisa, who can always find a few places to put red marks when editing my text. I also thank Bruce Corwin, friend, fellow artist, and grand tier of flies, for reviewing the tying segments of this book.

Bass Flies

Quill-Bodied Fly

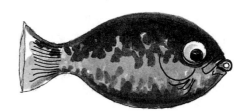

Bluegill Fly

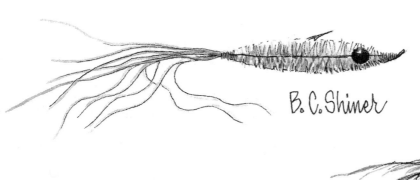

B. C. Shiner

Stir Stick
Damselfly

Floss Fly

Electrician's
Hellgrammite

Fishy's Foam Frog

Quill-Bodied Fly

While going through one of my old fly boxes, I discovered several Quill-Bodied Flies. My best guess was that I tied them back in the late seventies or early eighties, but I remember tying dozens of these creations twenty-five years earlier. Back in the fifties, I had a good supply of the larger quills needed to tie these flies. My great-grandfather always had a few geese on his farm. He considered them much better "watchdogs" than the four-legged kind. When one of these nasty birds was dressed for the pot, I got the feathers. I tied dozens of flies using a variety of goose feathers, but the quills from the large wing feathers were my favorite.

A flock of chickens always hung out between the barn and the house. These birds supplied fresh eggs, many a Sunday feast, and more feathers. My favorite chicken feathers came from the little bantam roosters, since their plumage was the better hackle available to me at that time, but the best feathers came from Papa's larger birds. He always had a few guinea fowl and several peacocks. It was their feathers that I used most often when tying the quill-bodied creations.

I have replaced some of the materials with more modern stuff when tying this pattern, but I still prefer to use the guinea fowl and peacock. A couple of the marvelous spotted feathers from a guinea hen are tied over the back of the fly, and the peacock herl is tied under the body to simulate the legs. To this day I prefer to tie with these materials, because they are what I used when I first tied this fly five decades ago.

Back in the fifties, I tied the goose quill onto the hook, then coated the thread with varnish and set it aside to dry overnight. The next day, I plugged the end of the quill with a small ball of cotton, and then sealed the end with a coat of airplane glue. After the wing and legs were completed, a little enamel paint finished the head and eyes. I have replaced the varnish with superglue, the airplane glue with five-minute epoxy, and the slow-drying enamel paint with fingernail polish. Even though I have made a few updates in my choice of materials, this fly looks very similar to the ones I tied as a youngster. Tie up a few in a variety of sizes and colors and fish them. The Quill-Bodied Fly may be an oldie, but it is fun to tie, and the fish still jump all over it.

Materials List

HOOK:	Any light-wire hook that accommodates the size of the quill body.
THREAD:	3/0 flat waxed nylon, your choice of color.
BODY:	Quill from any large wing or tail feather.
WING:	Guinea hen. Other small breast feathers may also be used.
LEGS:	Six to eight strands of peacock herl.
FINGERNAIL POLISH:	Used to complete the head and eyes.
SUPERGLUE:	Used to prevent the quill from twisting on the hook shank.
FIVE-MINUTE EPOXY:	Used to seal the open end of the quill.

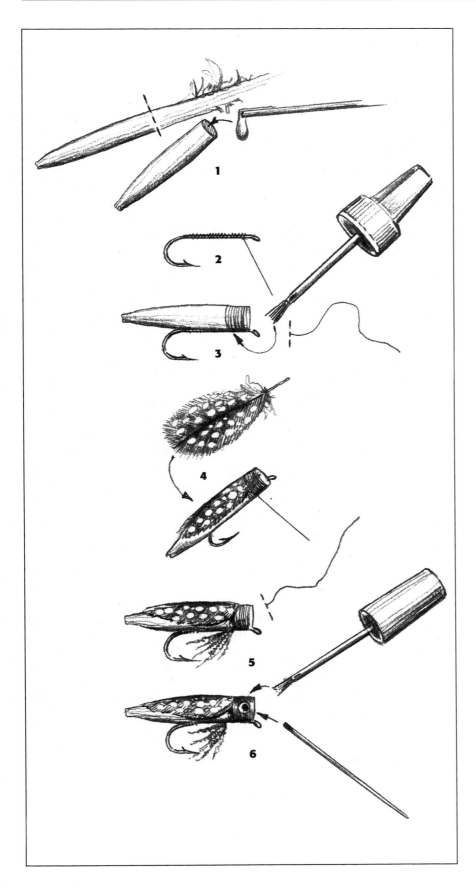

1. Cut a section of quill that fits the size of the fly you are tying. Seal the hollow end of the quill with a small amount of epoxy; if water seeps into the quill, the fly will not float.

2. Wrap the entire hook shank with thread.

3. Tie the quill to the hook, and tie off the thread. Apply a generous amount of superglue along the entire length of the hook shank. Coat the thread wraps with superglue.

4. Reattach the thread, and tie on the wing. The wing should lie across the back and along the sides of the quill body.

5. Tie in six to eight strands of peacock herl to simulate the legs, trim to size, and tie off the thread.

6. Paint the head and eyes using fingernail polish. Use a round toothpick to paint the center of the eye.

Fishy's Bluegill Fly

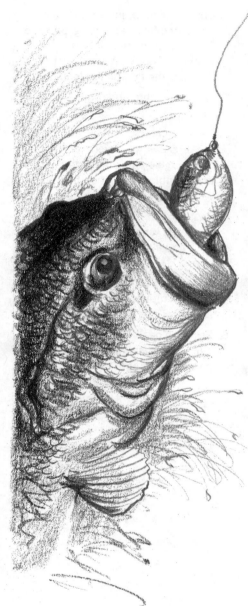

Late last spring, my grandson and I were having a wonderful time catching bluegills that had set up housekeeping along the far end of the pond. Most of the fish were averaging between seven and nine inches, and they were lots of fun on light rods. As another fish came up and inhaled his little popper, Tim reacted, setting the hook. But the instant the fish came to the surface, he was disappointed. It was a rather small fish, which he easily lifted into the canoe. Tim tried to remove the popper from the fish's mouth for several minutes, but the fish had taken the popper clear to its tail. He needed some help.

I had a fish on, and at the moment, it was refusing to come to the boat. A bass had taken my small popper, and it was going to be a while before I could help Tim, so I suggested that he return the small bluegill to the water. I finally landed the foot-long bass and turned to Tim, telling him to retrieve his fish. As he pulled the fish toward the boat, the water opened up, his rod doubled, and the light tippet parted. An enormous largemouth had taken the small fish off the surface. We no longer had to worry about unhooking the small bluegill.

Losing a small panfish to a bass was a first for my grandson, but I've had it happen to me dozens of times, especially when fishing this pond. This body of water is carefully managed to keep the predator-prey relationship between the bass and panfish in balance. We keep some of the panfish but return most of the bass, especially the larger fish. The bigger largemouth keep the number of panfish in check. If we kept the bigger bass, the panfish numbers would explode, the pond would soon be over-populated with thousands of stunted fish, and the quality of fishing for both bass and panfish would suffer.

Knowing that the larger residents of the pond commonly feed on the smaller panfish prompted me to design a bluegill fly that might attach a few of these lunkers onto the end of my line. I started out with some very large prototypes. I really wanted to offer the big bass a 4- or 5-inch bluegill imitation, but these huge creations didn't cast very well. In fact, they were nearly impossible to cast even with larger outfits. Reluctantly, I slowly reduced the size until the Bluegill Fly handled fairly well in the air.

This small bluegill imitation is fun to make, and the pattern holds up surprisingly well for a creation made from a discarded foam meat tray. I admit that from the angler's perspective, it doesn't look like much on the water, but the bass like it. If you cast it out near bassy-looking cover and give it a wiggle every minute or so, it often triggers a response from some of the larger bass. Make up a couple and give them a try.

Materials List

HOOK: #4/0 or, better yet, #5/0.

THREAD: 3/0 flat waxed nylon is used to prewrap the hook shank.

BODY: A piece cut out of the bottom of a recycled meat tray. Choose a heavier tray; it makes a more durable fly. Meat trays are usually available in black, white, or yellow. I used a yellow one for this particular pattern.

FINE SANDPAPER: Used to smooth the edges of the foam.

FIVE-MINUTE EPOXY: Used to secure the hook and eyes, and to coat the body before painting.

EYES: Round plastic doll eyes.

FINGERNAIL POLISH: Light green, brown, and orange are used to color the fly.

BLACK MARKER: Used to detail the gills, mouth, and tail of the bluegill.

1. Make a paper pattern (trace reference found in step 2 of painting instructions), and then transfer it onto the bottom of the meat tray with a fine tip black marking pen. Note that the tail is positioned over the bend.

2. Cut out the body using an X-acto knife.

3. With the tail pointing down, taper the edges and the end of the tail with the knife, and finish with fine sandpaper.

4. Turn the body so that the tail is pointing up, and cut a groove for the hook. Don't cut all the way through the foam; cut only halfway through.

5. Prewrap the hook shank with thread and tie off. Apply a little five-minute epoxy into the groove, and then force the hook into the foam. Add a little more epoxy over the area. Smooth it out, removing the excess, and set the fly aside to harden.

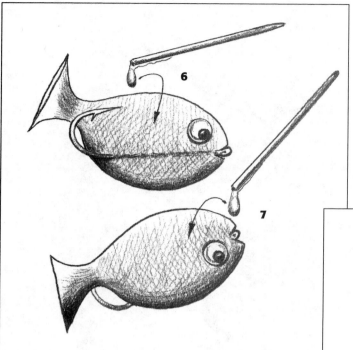

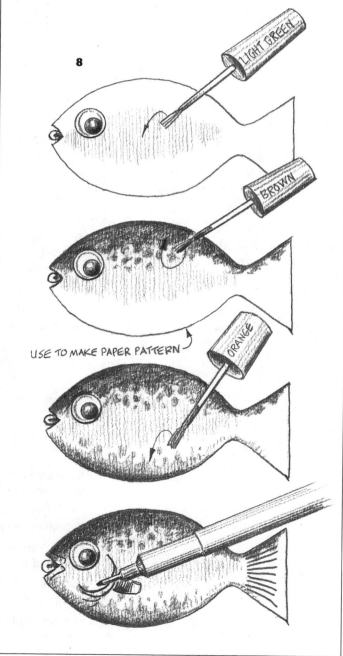

USE TO MAKE PAPER PATTERN

6. Using your finger or a small piece of soft foam, apply five-minute epoxy over the entire hook side of the fly. When the epoxy begins to harden, position one of the eyes.

7. Apply a thin coat of epoxy to the backside of the body, and position the other eye. Applying a thin coat of epoxy to the entire body makes the pattern more durable and prevents the paints from melting the foam.

8. Paint the Bluegill Fly with several different colors of fingernail polish. Use a black marker to add a little detail.

BC Shiner

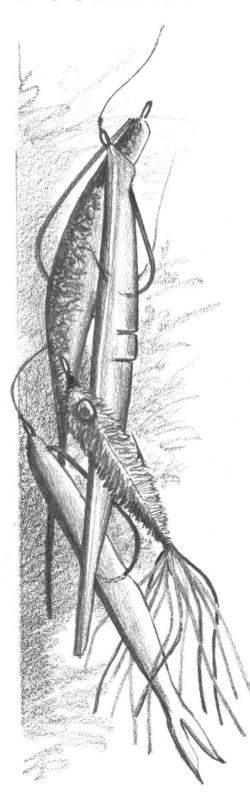

The vast majority of my fishing partners are primarily fly fishers. A few will occasionally pick up a spinning or bait-casting outfit, but most pursue everything from bluegills to bonefish with the long rod. Dick is the exception. Since the late summer of 1973, Dick Bengraff and I have spent countless days on the water in pursuit of various kinds of fish in both fresh and salt water. During that time, I have never seen him with a fly rod in hand. He prefers to cast lures made of lead and plastic rather than flies, affectionately referring to my efforts with the fly rod as "swish swish."

Over the years that we have fished together, Dick has tried to teach me how to rig and catch fish with a variety of smelly plastic baits, but I usually stay with my fly tackle. At times my flies did not stand up very well compared with his baits, and on numerous trips, Dick took many more fish than I was able to catch on fly tackle. Finally I decided that it was time to design a fly that resembled some of the plastic, minnowlike creations that were so productive. But coming up with a pattern that would copy the appearance, weedless quality, and action of the plastic baits turned out to be quite a challenge.

Recently, while working on another fly, I happened upon a design that looked like the plastic baits. After making up several prototypes and throwing them within reach of a few largemouth bass, I discovered that this new creation just might put me on par with those fishing the smelly plastic. For the first time, I could fish a fly that had the same qualities as the lures presented by this skillful spin fisherman.

Bump chenille can be made from one of two different materials, both common craft-store items. The kind made from a soft, cottonlike material is not usable for flies. I have even tried coating this softer material, but it just doesn't work well. The second kind is stiffer and tinsel-like, and that's the kind you need to use for this pattern. You might have to shop around a bit to find the right chenille, but it's worth it. The weedless quality of this fly makes the BC Shiner a very fishable addition to the bass angler's arsenal of flies.

Materials List

HOOK:	#3/0 straight-eye bass-bug hook.
THREAD:	White 3/0 flat waxed nylon.
BODY:	Any color of the stiffer, tinsel-like bump chenille.
TAIL:	Six or seven strands of Sili-Legs or other materials.
EYES:	Half-bead plastic or doll eyes (also found in craft stores).
HEAD CEMENT:	Used to complete the tail.
FIVE-MINUTE EPOXY:	Used to attach the eyes.
SUPERGLUE:	Used to prevent the body from twisting on the hook.
MARKERS:	Used to color the top of the fly.

1. Begin with half a piece of bump chenille, which will have two bumps in it. Bend the material at the narrow area between the bumps, and press the wire tightly together.

2. Attach thread to the narrow end of the chenille body. Position six or seven strands of Sili-Legs across the end of the body, and then make a couple wraps around the tail material.

3. Pull the strands of the tail back, make a few more wraps, and tie off the thread. A drop or two of head cement completes the tail.

4. Attach the eyes with five-minute epoxy. Let it harden, then apply a second thin coat over the eyes to make them more secure. You can squeeze the two sections of the body together when positioning the eyes, but keep the chenille separated while the epoxy is curing to avoid gluing the sections together. If this happens, the hook cannot be rigged inside the body. After the eyes are attached, trim the front of the chenille with a pair of wire cutters.

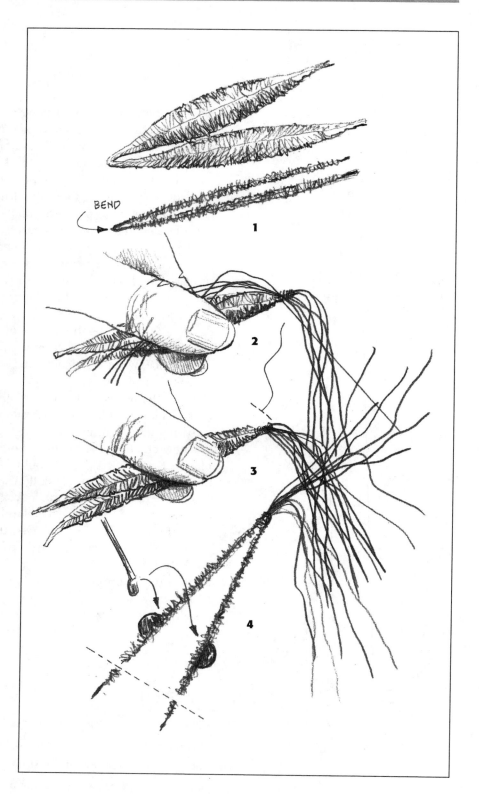

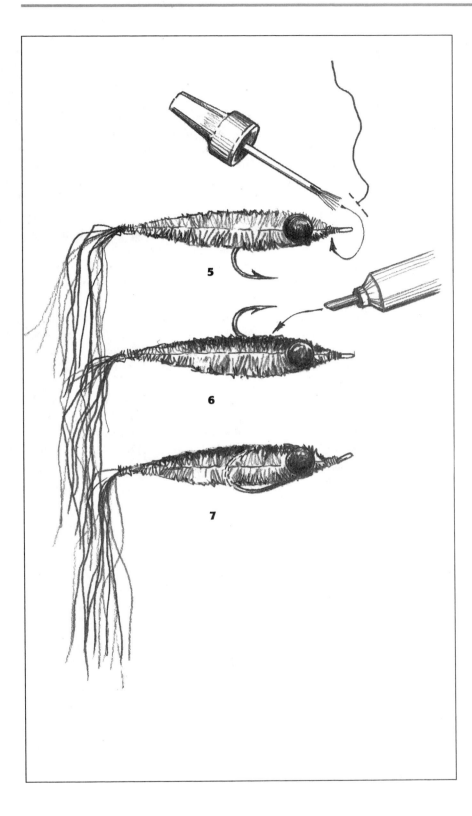

5. Put the hook in your fly-tying vise. Attach the thread, and position the body sections against either side of the hook, just behind the eye of the hook. Secure the body with fifteen to twenty wraps of thread and tie off. Complete the head by applying superglue over the entire thread, being careful not to get any glue on the body of the fly.

6. Color the top of the fly with whatever color markers you like. Note that the hook point is up.

7. After the head is dry, bend the body down slightly beyond the point of the hook. This positions the hook completely inside the body of the fly, making the BC Shiner just about snag-proof.

Stir-Stick Damselfly

Don't throw your plastic coffee stir sticks away; you can turn them into a very fishable fly. This is a great way to recycle an item that is normally discarded after a single use. Stir sticks come in many different colors and shapes. Some are round, resembling miniature drinking straws, and others are square. All may be used when tying this very productive damselfly pattern.

Fish seem to like damselfly imitations, making them productive fish catchers. If damselflies are flying back and forth over the surface of the water, you can be sure the fish are looking for the opportunity to capture and eat them. Panfish and bass may enjoy the challenge of the chase, or maybe it's the taste, but for whatever reason, they almost always will take one of these flies if given half a chance.

When I've seen damselflies struggling on the surface, I've paddled off a short distance and watched and waited. They don't last very long—their struggling soon brings a splashy response. Careful observation has always shown the natural with its head down and body pointing upward. I've never seen a live one lying flat in the surface film like a mayfly spinner. The Stir-Stick Damselfly rides with its body pointing upward, just like the real thing. The hollow air chamber keeps the body afloat, while the weight of the eyes and hook causes the head to sink slightly.

To fish this pattern, it is mostly wiggled in place rather than retrieved across the surface of the water. If a strike doesn't happen, cast to a new location, then put a little life back into the fly.

Materials List

HOOK:	#6 or #8, 2XL dry-fly hook.
THREAD:	6/0 brown or black.
BODY:	A plastic coffee stir stick.
THORAX:	Brown dubbing fur.
EYES:	Black plastic beads.
WING:	Fine white bucktail.
LEGS:	Brown hackle fibers.
SUPERGLUE:	Used to secure the body and eyes.

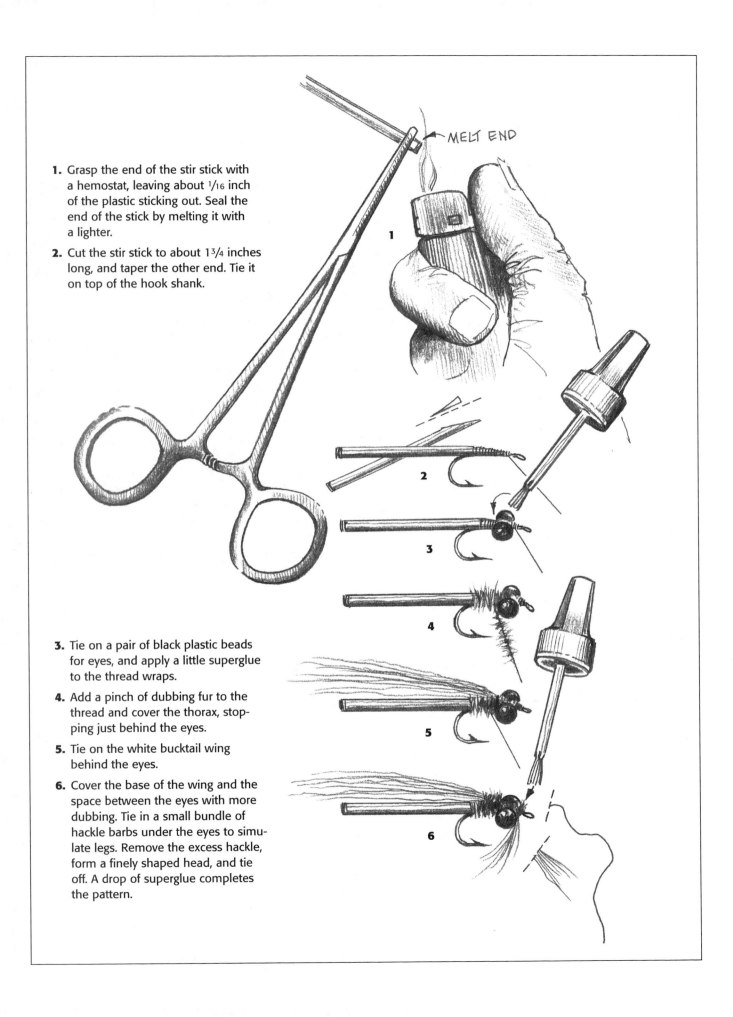

1. Grasp the end of the stir stick with a hemostat, leaving about 1/16 inch of the plastic sticking out. Seal the end of the stick by melting it with a lighter.

2. Cut the stir stick to about 1 3/4 inches long, and taper the other end. Tie it on top of the hook shank.

3. Tie on a pair of black plastic beads for eyes, and apply a little superglue to the thread wraps.

4. Add a pinch of dubbing fur to the thread and cover the thorax, stopping just behind the eyes.

5. Tie on the white bucktail wing behind the eyes.

6. Cover the base of the wing and the space between the eyes with more dubbing. Tie in a small bundle of hackle barbs under the eyes to simulate legs. Remove the excess hackle, form a finely shaped head, and tie off. A drop of superglue completes the pattern.

MELT END

Floss Fly

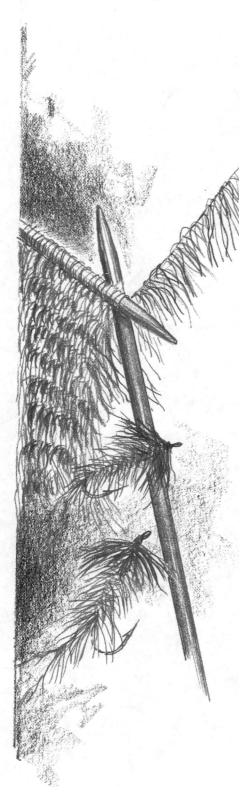

I am constantly searching the craft stores for something that might turn out to be a practical addition to my somewhat unusual inventory of fly-tying materials. During a recent visit, my wife suggested that I look at some of the new yarns in a different part of the store. There were hundreds of kinds of conventional yarns, but Carol had found some amazing new ones. After looking at dozens of these bizarre yarns, I decided to purchase a skein each of Fun Fur and Rave. A length of these yarns looks similar to a sparse dubbing loop, but the yarn loop is made up of hundreds of strands of embroidery floss rather than fur or hair.

Minutes after returning home, I was at the vise. I attached several strands of the Fun Fur to the rear of a streamer hook, and then tied in a length of the Rave yarn at the base of the tail. As I wound the yarn around the hook, I pulled the strands of floss back, trying not to capture the strands under the next wrap. After covering about three-quarters of the hook shank, I tied off the yarn and trimmed the body, tapering it slightly toward the rear. A couple wraps of the Fun Fur completed the front of the body. After tying off, I applied a drop of superglue to secure the head. After the glue was dry, I gave the fly a final trim.

The Floss Fly is a very simple pattern to tie. It's extremely durable, it has great action in the water, and the multiple colors look great. Besides Fun Fur and Rave, there are dozens of other, similar yarns that would also work for this fly. See what's available at your local craft store. You can try different brands and colors, vary the size of the fly, trim to different shapes, and add other materials. Have fun with some of these strange, wonderful yarns.

Materials List

HOOK: #4 or #6 streamer hook.

THREAD: Brown or black 6/0.

TAIL AND BODY: Fun Fur and Rave, or any other yarns made from strands of embroidery floss.

SUPERGLUE OR HEAD CEMENT: Used to secure the head.

1. Attach the thread. Tie two or three short lengths of Fun Fur at the rear of the hook to form the tail.

2. Tie in a length of Rave yarn at the base of the tail.

3. Wrap the Rave yarn forward. As you work, pull the floss strands back to avoid capturing them under the next wraps of yarn. Cover about three-quarters of the hook shank to form the body of the fly. Tie off and clip the excess.

4. Tie on another length of Fun Fur in front of the body.

5. Wrap the Fun Fur yarn forward, again pulling the strands back out of the way. When you reach the head, tie off the yarn and remove the excess. Finish off the head, tie off the thread, and then add a drop or two of superglue or head cement.

6. Allow the glue to dry, and then give the fly a final trim.

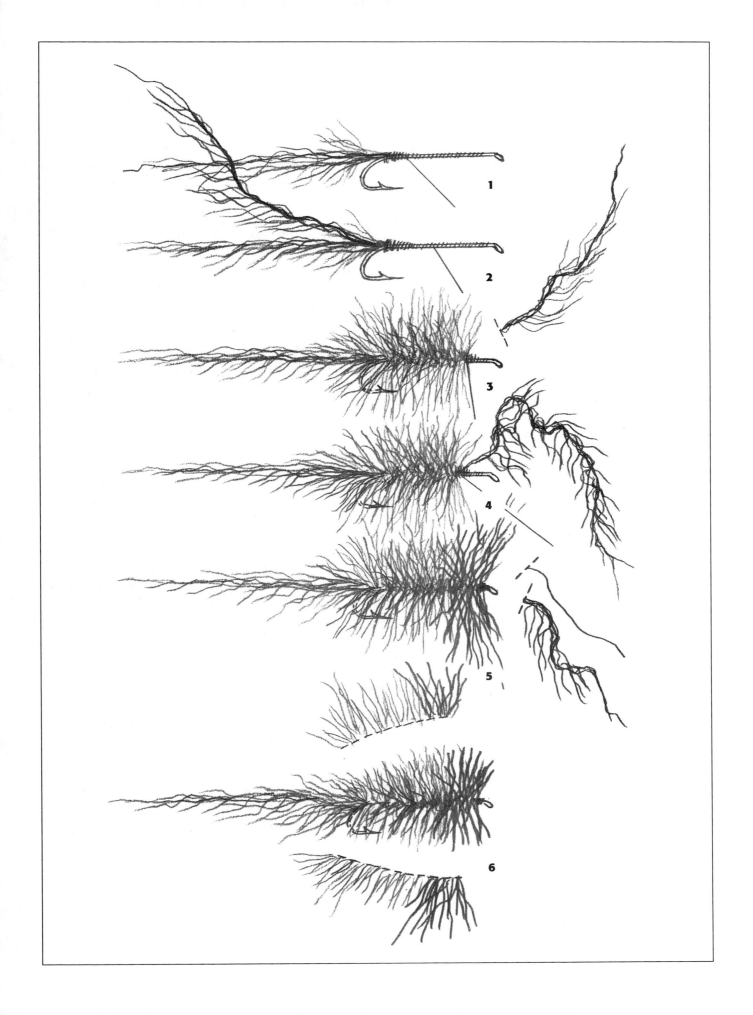

1

2

3

4

5

6

Fishy's Foam Frog

Most of the time I prefer to cut and shape my own foam bodies, but after completing the design for this nifty little frog pattern, I've decided that Bill's precut bodies work the best. Bill Skilton is a very skilled and innovative tier who has developed and marketed dozens of great foam products. He introduced me to a new foam body at one of the fly shows last year, and I finally found the time to see if this new product could be transformed into something the fish would eat.

The basic shape of the new body is similar to Bill's hopper bodies, but it is cut out of much thicker foam. It looks like several hopper bodies that have been glued together. When I started out I wasn't quite sure what to do with it, but attaching the foam block to a hook was a good start. I made a cut along the center of the body, about halfway through the foam. I then prewrapped a hook with thread, forced the hook into the foam and secured it with superglue.

Shortly after clamping the hook into the vise, I determined that the foam body resembled the body of a frog, but the shape needed a little work. I cut a length of 3/0 thread off the spool and wrapped it around the foam body a couple of times, about a third of the way from the front, then pulled hard on both ends of the thread. The thread formed the head of the frog, greatly improving the overall shape of the body. I then applied a thin coat of five-minute epoxy under the belly of the frog. After the epoxy hardened, I painted the belly with yellow fingernail polish.

I tried several different types of eyes, finally deciding on small pom-poms glued to either side of the body. I then used waterproof marking pens to color the body and eyes. All that was left were the legs. I knew exactly how they would be attached to the body, but I tried several materials before finding one that did the job. The first attempts failed because the material broke as I attempted to pull it through the rear of the body using a large sewing needle. Spanflex worked on five of the six prototypes. I had to redo one because I got in a hurry when finishing the last pair of legs.

I tied off the legs at the ankles with several wraps of thread on some of the prototypes, and then applied a drop of superglue to secure the thread. This made the legs look more lifelike in the water, but the jointed legs have a tendency to tangle around the hook. Legs that simply splay out on either side and behind the frog are a little less apt to tangle. You might try both types of legs and decide which you prefer.

This small Foam Frog looks like the real thing as it is retrieved along the surface of the water. I have done very well fishing it during the past few months. The bass just love it; consequently, it has quickly become one of Fishy's Favorites.

Materials List

HOOK: A bass-bug hook with a shank that is slightly shorter than the body of the frog. I use #4 bass-bug hooks with the regular size bodies, #2 for the jumbo bodies.

THREAD: Prewrap the hook shank with any 6/0 thread. 3/0 flat waxed is used to shape the body.

BODY: Bill Skilton's light green, tan, or yellow frog foam. The blanks come in two sizes (regular and jumbo); both make great frogs. If you can't find the bodies at your local fly shop, contact Bill at USA-Flies, P.O. Box 64, Boiling Springs, PA 17007, or give him a call at (717) 258-0642. You can also cut your own bodies from the foam blocks or from thicker sheets of dense foam found at your local craft store. The size of the regular body is 1/2" x 3/16" x 1 1/4". Jumbo bodies are 1/2" x 1/4" x 1 1/2".

EYES: Tan 5mm pom-poms. Small doll eyes or paint also work.

LEGS: Tan or green Spanflex. Thin rubber bands are a great substitute.

FIVE-MINUTE EPOXY: Used to coat the belly and to secure the eyes.

NEEDLE: Used to attach the legs.

SUPERGLUE: Used to secure the body to the hook and to coat the thread if you joint the legs.

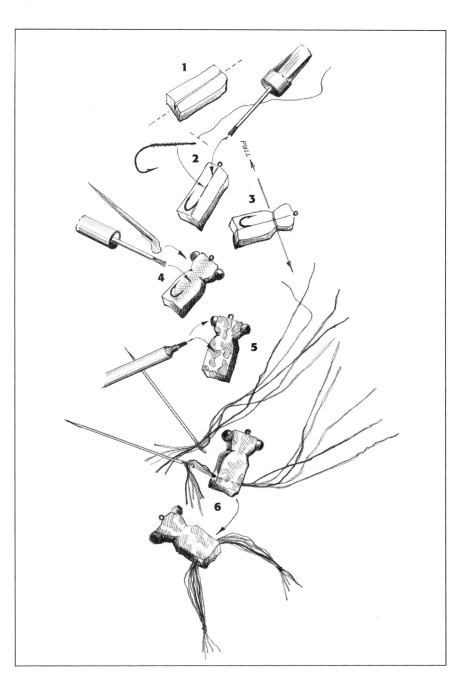

1. Cut a groove along the center of the foam body, cutting *halfway* through the foam.

2. Prewrap the hook shank with thread, then force it into the foam body. Use superglue to secure the hook to the body.

3. Make two wraps of 3/0 thread around the body a third of the way back from the front, then pull hard on both ends of the thread to shape the body. Tie a knot under the body, then remove the excess thread.

4. Coat the belly of the frog with five-minute epoxy. Use a little of the same epoxy to attach the pom-pom eyes. After the epoxy has hardened, paint the belly of the frog with light green or yellow fingernail polish.

5. Color the body and the eyes with waterproof markers.

6. Thread five strands of Spanflex through the eye of a large sewing needle, then push the needle through the rear the body. Pull the material through the body, and then pull on the material to adjust the length. Legs can then be jointed at the ankles, or not. It's your choice.

Electrician's Hellgrammite

Long before I developed any proficiency at fishing artificial flies, I used a wide variety of live baits. Catching the bait was often as much fun as tempting the fish with it. I netted and trapped minnows, caught frogs with my bare hands, dug worms, and picked night crawlers. When going after smallmouth bass, I sometimes fished minnows or worms, but my favorite baits were crayfish and hellgrammites. The smallmouth liked the crayfish, and they were easier to handle than the hellgrammites. If I kept a firm grip on either side of the thorax, they were unable to pinch me with their claws.

Although the live hellgrammites were absolutely, positively the best bait any fisherman could thread on a hook when fishing for smallmouth, it wasn't easy to do so. Each time I reached into my bait box for another hellgrammite, it was a toss-up as to who was going to grab whom. More often than not, those nasty pincers would nip me, resulting in a painful pinch and the loss of a drop or two of blood. Looking back at my experience with these mean critters, I wonder if the hellgrammite was one of the reasons why I decided to fish with flies rather than live bait.

I haven't fished a real live hellgrammite in many years, but I still remember that the smallmouth preferred these creatures to any of the other live baits I offered them. These days, I occasionally attach a hellgrammite to a hook, but one that is securely held in the jaws of my fly-tying vise. These hellgrammites are created from a variety of tying materials, and then stored in a fly box rather than a bait box. This imitation triggers strikes almost as well as the real thing, and the Electrician's Hellgrammites usually don't draw blood like the ones with those nasty pincers, though you need to be careful when tying them onto presharpened hooks.

Materials List

HOOK: #4, 6XL streamer.

THREAD: Black 6/0.

TOP OF ABDOMEN: Black electrician's tape.

RIB: Green rod-wrapping thread, size D or E, or Kevlar.

ABDOMEN (UNDERBODY): Woolly Bugger Chenille (available from Bill Skilton's USA-Flies).

PINCERS: Small black hackles.

EYES: Black bead chain.

LEGS: Soft black saddle hackle.

THORAX: Coarse medium gray dubbing covered with five-minute epoxy, which is painted with brown fingernail polish.

SOFT BLACK HACKLE: Used to simulate legs.

SUPERGLUE: Used to prevent eyes from twisting.

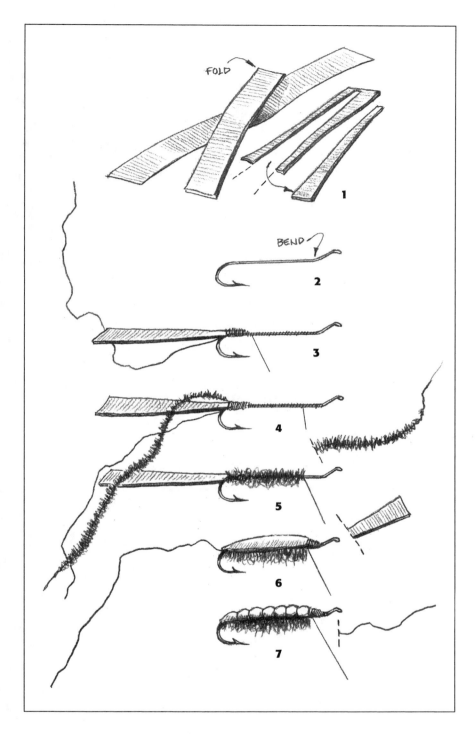

1. Cut a 5- to 6-inch length of black electrician's tape from the roll, fold it in half, and stick the sticky sides together. Cut a tapered strip from the piece that is slightly longer than the length of the hook.

2. Bend the hook shank slightly upward.

3. Attach the thread, then tie on a 9- to 10-inch length of heavy green thread (size D or E) or Kevlar to the rear of the hook. Tie in the tapered piece of electrician's tape.

4. Tie in the Woolly Bugger Chenille.

5. Wrap the chenille forward, covering at least three-quarters of the hook shank. Tie it off and remove the excess.

6. Pull the tape forward, and secure it just ahead of the chenille. Tie off the tape and clip off the excess.

7. Wrap the green thread forward to form the rib. Pick out the strands of chenille with your bodkin as you wrap. Tie off the ribbing and remove the excess. It is important to have strands of chenille extending out along both sides of the body.

8. Tie in a pair of small black hackles just behind the eye of the hook. Trim the hackles to look like the hellgrammite's nasty pincers.

9. Tie in a pair of black bead-chain eyes. Add a drop of superglue to prevent the eyes from twisting.

10. Tie in a soft black hackle for legs, then cover the thorax with a coarse medium gray dubbing.

11. Wrap the hackle forward (palmer style) and tie it off. Remove the excess, and tie off the thread. Complete this step by removing all of the hackle from the top of the thorax.

12. Coat the top of the thorax with five-minute epoxy. After the epoxy has hardened, paint the area with brown fingernail polish. Taper the chenille along both sides of the body to complete the pattern.

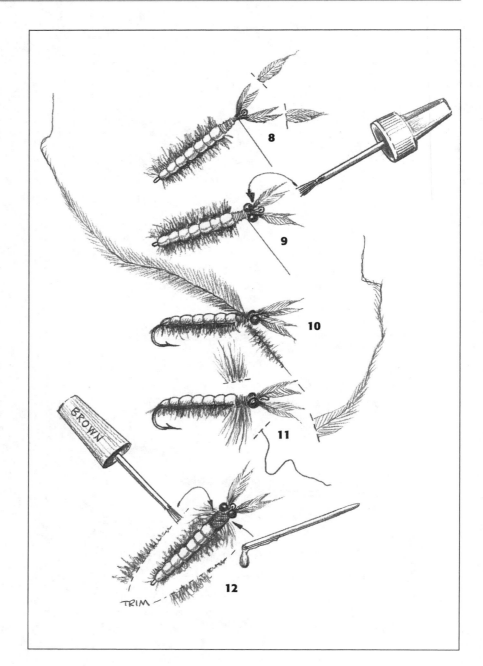

Trout Flies

Early Hopper

Itsy Bitsy Spider

Foam Inchworm

U.V. Nymph

P.F.D. Dry Fly

Small Fry

Easy-Parachute

Floating Soft Hackle

Baggy Nymph

Extended-Body Dry

Midnight Snack

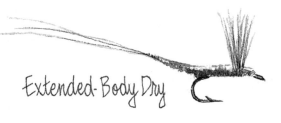

Itsy Bitsy Spider

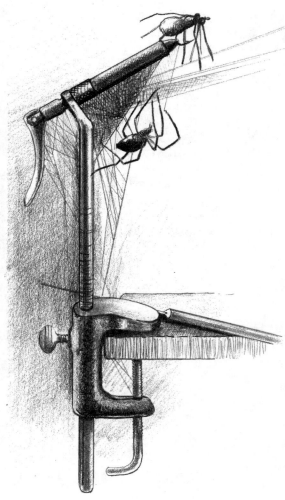

While fishing one of the local streams late last summer, I stopped to take a break and replace a very short tippet. As I sat completing the second half of the blood knot, I noticed a large spider on the water. As it scampered across the surface, it attracted the attention of one of the spotted residents of the pool. Seconds later, the brown trout took the spider and disappeared. I clipped off the tag ends and reattached my fly, making a mental note to add a spider to my growing inventory of terrestrials. Many of the trout I had caught during the past few seasons, including some of the better fish, were taken on Foam Hoppers, Early Hoppers, Epoxy Ants, Inchworms, and beetle imitations, but arachnids were also out there in great numbers. Designing a much-needed spider was long overdue.

I thought that designing a simple, realistic spider pattern would be an easy task. A spider is just a body, eyes, and some long, spindly legs. How hard could it be? I worked on this pattern for weeks. The eyes and legs were no-brainers, but I could not come up with a body that looked like a spider.

Then, during a fly-fishing show, I was working at the vise on my spider pattern. Earlier that afternoon, one of my fishing partners had stopped by with a sandwich and a cold drink. Still struggling with the spider body, I pulled a little dubbing fur from an envelope. Just as I was about to spin the dubbing around the thread, the plastic wrap around the sandwich caught my eye. I cut a small piece of the sandwich wrap, rolled the dubbing fur in my fingers, placed the ball in the center of the wrap, and folded the plastic around it. Even before I tied it onto the top of the hook shank, I knew I had solved my problem.

The dubbing ball and small piece of plastic wrap combine to make a very realistic spider body. Maybe too realistic. I recently tied the Itsy Bitsy Spider during a fly-tying demo in New Jersey. After completing the pattern, I removed it from the vise and held it out so that the man in front of me could see it better. The youngster next to him took one look at the spider and ran.

The trout also seem to think it's the real thing. I've done very well with this pattern, as the fish love it. The Itsy Bitsy Spider is a welcome addition to my growing inventory of terrestrials. I strongly suggest that you add a few of these spiders to your box.

Materials List

HOOK:	#14 regular dry-fly hook.
THREAD:	6/0 or 8/0; match the color to the dubbing fur.
BODY:	Gray, tan, brown, or black dubbing fur covered with a thin, clear plastic. The plastic bags used by dry cleaners to protect clothing work great.
TYING WAX:	Makes forming the dubbing ball easier.
EYES:	Small, black plastic bead chain (common craft store item).
LEGS:	Sili-Legs or any other synthetic legs.
SUPERGLUE:	Used to prevent the body and eyes from twisting on the hook shank.

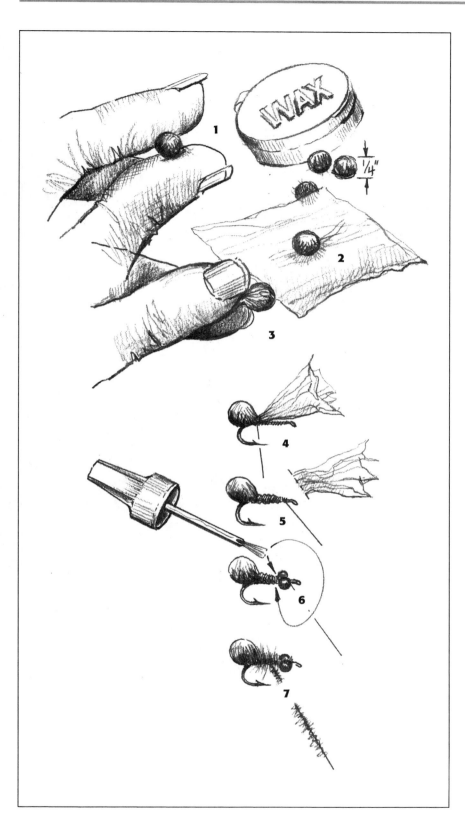

1. Roll a small bunch of dubbing fur into a ¼ inch-diameter ball. Applying a little tying wax to your fingers makes it easier to form the dubbing ball.

2. Place the ball on a small piece of thin, clear plastic.

3. Fold the plastic around the dubbing to form the spider's body.

4. Attach the thread, and wrap a thin layer around the entire length of the hook shank. Then tie on the body so that it extends slightly behind the rear of the hook.

5. Remove as much of the excess plastic as possible with your scissors. Make additional wraps of thread to cover any remaining plastic.

6. Tie on the eyes. Apply a little super-glue along the bottom of the hook shank and between the eyes.

7. Using the same dubbing, cover the rest of the body and figure-eight to fill the space between the eyes.

8. Fold the leg material around the thread. Maintaining light pressure on the leg material and thread, slide the base of the legs up to the back of the eyes, and secure with several wraps of thread.

9. Rotate the hook in the vise, and then attach the legs on the other side of the spider. Tie off the thread and add a drop of superglue.

10. Trim the legs to the desired length to complete the Itsy Bitsy Spider.

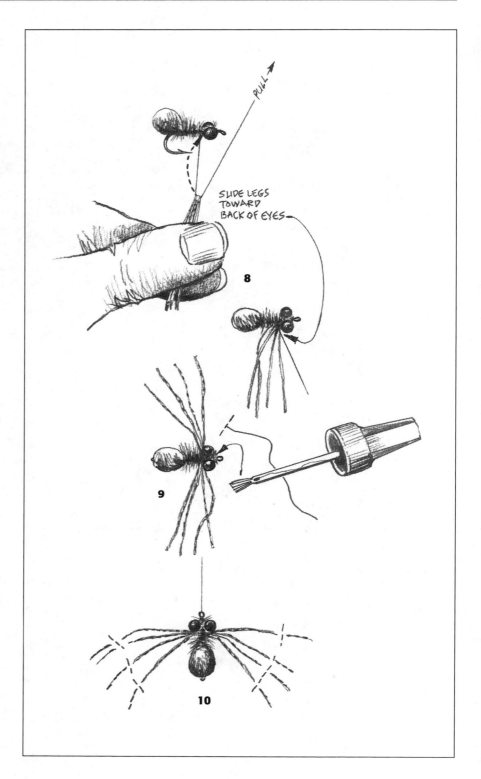

Early Hopper

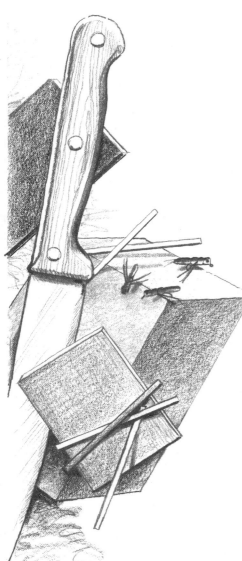

I designed the Foam Hopper specifically for a Montana trip in the fall of 1996. During this marvelous two-week adventure, I took many fine trout on the new pattern. It turned out to be an excellent imitation when the adult red-legged grasshoppers were on the water.

After returning home, I continued to experiment with the hopper pattern. By the following spring, I had accumulated dozens of prototypes. Most of my new creations were larger than the original Foam Hopper, but after fishing these larger hoppers an entire season, I discovered that the trout didn't particularly like them. Although the Foam Hopper tied on a #8 nymph hook was fine, larger creations were often refused, with one exception: The larger hoppers were a better choice when fishing for bass. This was not because these fish preferred a larger bite, but because the increased size of the hook gap improved my hooking percentage.

After going through my large hopper phase, I began tying smaller and smaller hoppers. The small hoppers were amazing. The trout loved them. I have fished the small Early Hoppers for eight seasons and have caught hundreds of browns, brooks, and rainbows on these creations.

Several years after an article on the Foam Hoppers was published in *Fly Tyer* magazine in autumn 1997, I did a second article on the smaller Early Hoppers (summer 2000), in which I explained that these represented immature hoppers and could be fished long before adult hoppers were available to the fish. Looking back now, I wish I had established this pattern as a small bug rather than a baby grasshopper. If I had offered this pattern as another valuable terrestrial rather than an immature grasshopper, I believe more fly fishers would have tied and fished it.

Sure, I fish the Early Hoppers when I find good numbers of immature grasshoppers along the stream, but I fish the smaller ones (#14 to #18) during the entire season. Dozens of grasshopper species are found regionally throughout the country, but there are more than thirty thousand beetle species. With one of these smaller flies tied onto my tippet, I am more often presenting a beetle imitation to the fish than a young grasshopper.

The Early Hopper is basically the same terrestrial pattern as the Foam Hopper, featured in my book *Fishy's Flies,* but tied smaller and without the wings. So why am I including the Early Hopper here? I actually have two very good reasons. First off, it is one of the most productive patterns I've ever tied onto the end of a tippet. And second, I've changed the body material and improved the tying technique.

Early Hoppers can be made from many different colors of foam. Bright green, tan, brown, and black are my favorites. A fellow tier introduced me to the Wapsi foam blocks, and I have used this foam for all of my smaller terrestrials ever since. It is much more durable than other foams, comes in a variety of great colors, and is very tier friendly.

Materials List

HOOK:	#12 to #16, 2XL dry-fly hook.
THREAD:	6/0, in a color that is either lighter or darker than the foam, so that the thread helps segment the body.
BODY:	Cut slices off the end of a block of Wapsi foam with a sharp knife, and cut them into square sticks of a size appropriate for the fly you're tying.
FIVE-MINUTE EPOXY:	Used to secure the body to the hook and make the pattern more durable.
LEGS:	Sili-Legs, nymph size, same color as the body.
FINGERNAIL POLISH:	Color of the body for the belly and black for the eyes.
WATERPROOF MARKERS:	Used to color the sides and top of the fly.
NEEDLE:	Used to attach the legs.

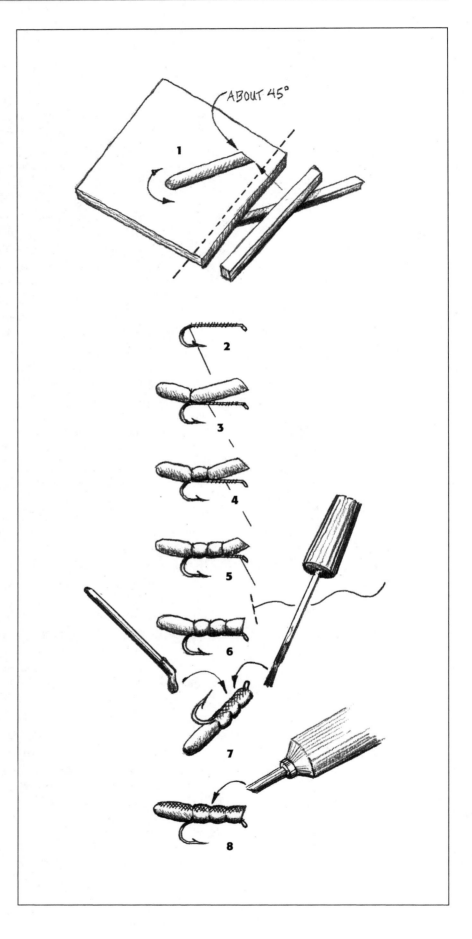

1. Cut the foam to shape. Match the size of the body to the hook you have chosen. Taper the head, and then trim the other end of the body to a rounded point.

2. Attach the thread and wrap the hook shank, stopping at the bend of the hook.

3. Hold the foam on the top of the hook, and make a couple wraps around the shank and body. Lift the front of the body enough to let you advance the thread one-third of the way forward along the hook shank.

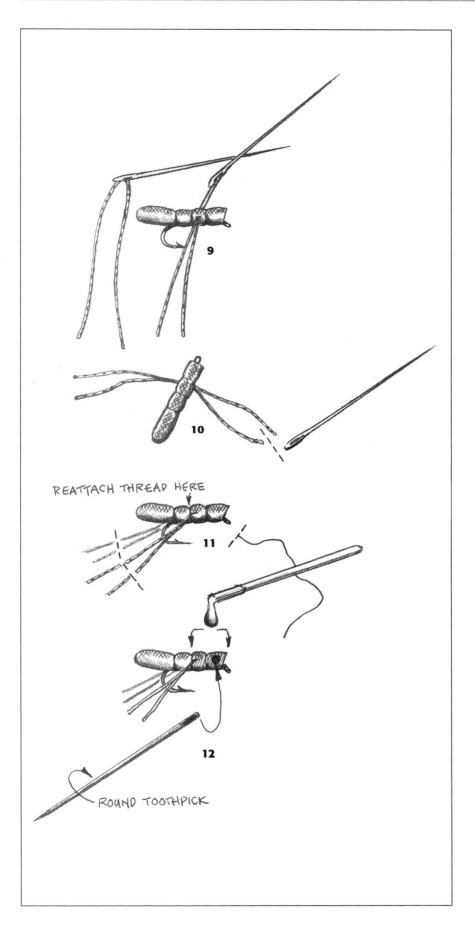

REATTACH THREAD HERE

ROUND TOOTHPICK

4. Make several wraps of thread around the body, then lift the front of the body and advance the thread. The thread should now be hanging from a point two-thirds of the way along the hook shank.

5. Make several more wraps around the body, and then advance the thread forward, stopping just behind the eye.

6. Secure the end of the tapered head to the front of the hook, and tie off.

7. Secure the belly of the foam to the hook with a little five-minute epoxy. After the epoxy has hardened, paint over the epoxy with fingernail polish that matches the color of the body.

8. Color the sides and top of the pattern with waterproof markers. Use your imagination; small terrestrials come in a wide variety of colors.

9. Thread a strand of Sili-Legs material through the eye of a needle, and then push the needle through the middle of the second segment of the body.

10. Free the needle by cutting the leg material; you now have two legs sticking out of each side of the foam.

11. Reattach the thread at the rear of the second segment. Hold the legs back along the sides of the body, make a couple soft wraps to secure them, and tie off. (If thread is pulled too tight, the legs will flare away from the body.) Don't worry about the durability of this band of thread; it's going to be coated with epoxy. Trim the legs to length.

12. Apply a thin coat of five-minute epoxy along the sides and the top of the head, covering the foam back to the band of thread that secured the legs. After the epoxy has hardened, paint the eyes with black fingernail polish.

Foam Inchworm

Like most stream trout fishers, I am always looking for fish rising to a particular adult aquatic insect. The trout's food supply can be either aquatic or terrestrial, however, and every time the wind blows through the canopy, thousands of land-dwelling insects and spiders are deposited onto the surface of our trout waters. If the wind is blowing and there are no aquatics on the water, I usually open one of my terrestrial boxes for something to tie onto the end of a leader.

It was dead calm and slightly overcast one afternoon, and a decent hatch was coming off. Terrestrials were the last things on my mind. My partner and I fished over the rising trout for nearly an hour without catching a single one. I had tried a few damp and wet patterns and a dozen different dry flies, but nothing was working. Finally I decided that it was time to stop and take a fresh look at what these annoying fish were doing. As I sat watching the trout, I noticed that their feeding seemed to be concentrated in three areas of the long run. I suddenly realized that these feeding areas were directly under the canopy.

I slowly inched my way upstream for a closer look. As I sat staring at the water, the sun happened to break through the clouds for a minute or two, lighting up the threads of dozens of tiny inchworms as they rappelled down to the waiting trout. The fish were feeding on the terrestrials, totally ignoring the mayflies.

Inchworms don't fall into the water like other terrestrials. These small caterpillars from the family Geometridae (measuring moths) descend from the canopy on strands of silk. After reaching the ground, they pupate. When they emerge as adults, the moths fly up into the trees and lay their eggs on the foliage, starting the cycle over again. During the late summer and early fall, thousands of these small caterpillars dangle from tree branches that just happen to be over the water. When this happens, they end up as trout food. If the inchworms are present in good numbers, the trout often become very selective, refusing everything but these lime green mouthfuls.

Materials List

HOOK:	#16 to #20, 2XL dry-fly hook.
THREAD:	Black 6/0 or 8/0.
BODY:	Lime green closed-cell foam from a kickboard used in swimming pools. If you can't find green, use yellow foam and color it with a light green waterproof marker.
SUPERGLUE:	Used to secure the body to the hook after tying it into place.
EYES:	Black fingernail polish.

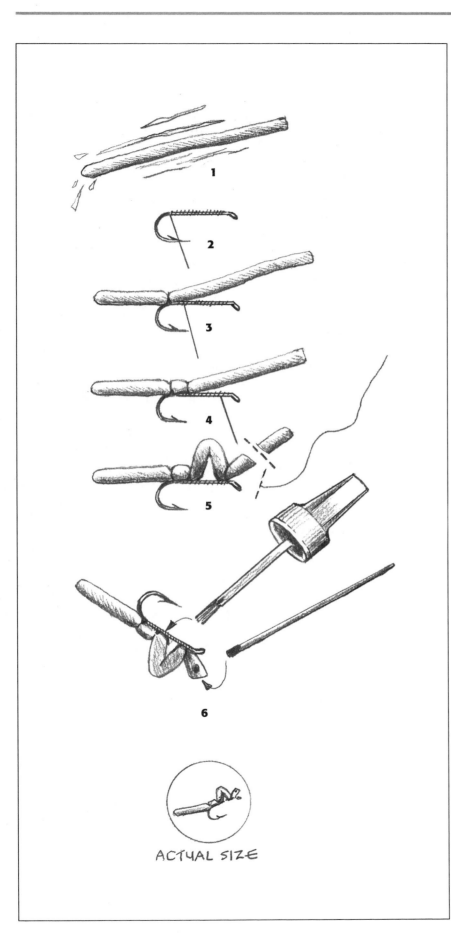

ACTUAL SIZE

1. Use a sharp knife to cut a long narrow length of foam. Carefully round the corners and butt end of the foam with scissors.

2. Attach the thread, then cover the entire hook shank with a thin layer of thread.

3. Position the foam on top of the hook, and make several soft wraps. Don't put too much pressure on the thread, or you might cut the foam. After securing the foam, advance the thread forward.

4. Make several more soft wraps around the foam, and then advance the thread forward, stopping slightly behind the hook eye.

5. Push the foam back to form a hump in the inchworm's body, and make several wraps around the foam. Remove the excess, then advance the thread and tie off behind the hook eye.

6. Coat the thread and the bottom of the foam with superglue. After the glue is dry, paint on the eyes with black fingernail polish.

PFD Dry Fly

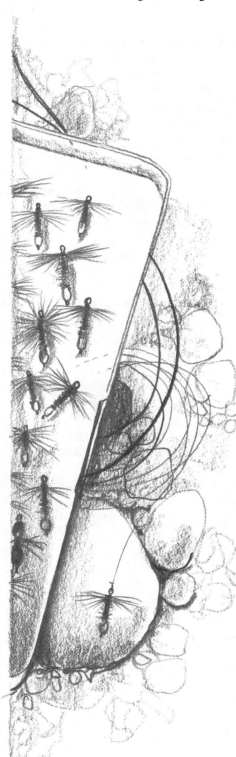

My supply of productive dry flies was growing thin. The previous afternoon, I had offered several flies to the tree gods, left another in the jaw of a sizable brown trout, and gave at least a dozen to my fishing partners. Following a hearty breakfast, a dozen fish stories, and several cups of strong coffee, we cleared the large, round table in the main room of the lodge and began a fly-tying session.

After tying a couple dozen traditional patterns, I went into my design mode. The previous day, I had seen thousands of adult mayflies traveling upstream, carrying their precious masses of bright yellow eggs. I put a hook in the vise, attached the thread, and tied on the tail. After tying in a post, I began looking through my tying stuff for something that was a bright yellow. The only thing I could find was a small plastic bag filled with pieces of yellow foam.

I tied a small piece of the foam back off the bend of the hook, advanced the thread a couple turns, then pulled the foam forward and made several more wraps. The foam looked like the eggs I'd seen the mayflies carrying, so I completed the body and hackle and tied it off. Before the next fish story ended, I had added six more of the flies to my inventory.

The hatches had been wonderful for the past three days, with lots of bugs and fish taking them. Returning to our favorite stretch of water, we sat and waited for things to happen. Conditions seemed to be the same, but there were very few mayflies on the water and even fewer fish taking them. After unsuccessfully fishing the standard pattern for nearly an hour, I decided it was time for a change. I selected a dry tied with the bright yellow foam and presented it to the trout. The first two times I drifted the fly down through the run, nothing happened. On the third attempt, a good fish came up and ate the fly. Catching a single fish didn't really prove anything, but after hooking and landing my third trout, I was beginning to think that maybe I had a winner.

Since that trip, I've included a bit of bright yellow foam on several more of my favorite dry flies. I'm convinced that adding the foam greatly improves many of these traditional patterns. Because the foam is tied directly above the heaviest part of the hook, it acts like a personal flotation device (PFD), keeping the fly afloat as it drifts along in the surface film. The PFD Drys are often more effective than standard flies because they float in the surface film rather than on top of the water. I believe this is why they often produce when similar dry-fly patterns are refused.

Materials List

HOOK: #16 or larger standard dry-fly hook. (The addition of the foam doesn't work very well on flies smaller than #16.)

THREAD: 6/0 or 8/0, matching color to the pattern tied.

EGGS: Soft, yellow kickboard foam.

TAIL, BODY, WING, AND HACKLE: Match to the particular dry-fly pattern you are tying.

HEAD CEMENT: Used to finish the head.

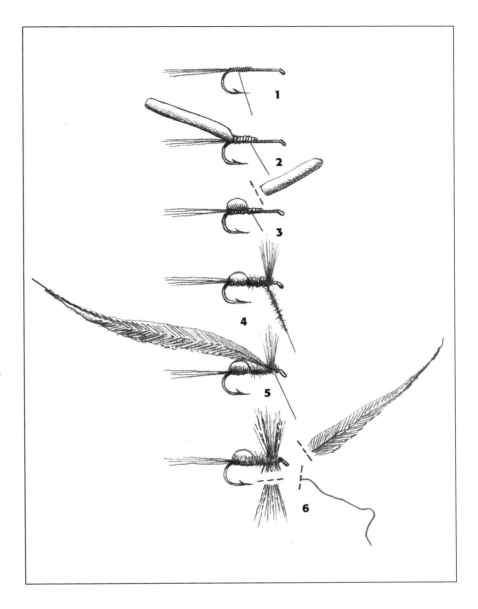

1. Attach the thread and tie in the tail.

2. Secure the foam at the back of the hook so it extends off the bend.

3. Pull the foam forward, and then make several thread wraps to attach the front of the foam piece securely to the hook. Clip the excess.

4. Tie in the wings, and cover the body with dubbing.

5. Select a hackle and tie it in at the base of the wing.

6. Wrap the hackle on either side of the wing, then tie off and remove the excess. Finish the head and tie off the thread. Add a drop of head cement to complete the pattern. I prefer to trim the hackle flat under the hook, but it's up to you.

UV Nymph

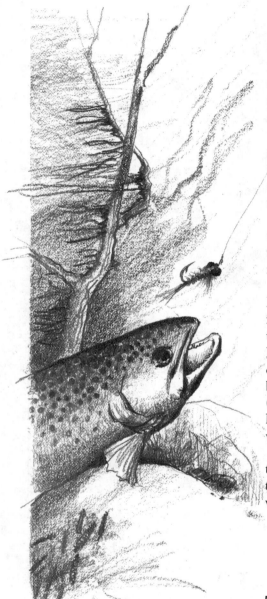

I was first introduced to UV Knot Sense soon after purchasing a new fly line. After the store owner attached the line to the backing, he coated the knot with the stuff, then instructed me to walk outside with him, where he exposed the area to the sun. In seconds it was cured, forming a smooth transition between the fly line and backing. Before leaving the fly shop, I purchased a tube of the new product so that I might coat the connections on other lines.

Before I began working on the other lines, I decided that it might be a good idea to read the directions printed on the side of the tube. The directions recommended the product for a number of uses, including repair of damaged flies. An hour later, I was at the vise experimenting with this new addition to my ever-growing inventory.

I have used this product over the backs of scuds and small shrimp patterns and to coat the foam bodies of my ant patterns. I have even used it to coat small popper bodies, but my favorite UV pattern is a variation of my Bead-Chain Nymph.

I was never satisfied with the look of the wing pad on the original BC Nymph. Using a tiny bit of the UV Knot Sense is a lot quicker, and the finished nymph looks much better. The wing pad on this nymph now takes only a few seconds to complete. I apply a small amount of the UV Knot Sense to the top of the head, and then spread the stuff over the top of the head, the eyes, and about a third of the body with the point of my bodkin. After the wing pad is completed, I use the handy little UV light (available from the same manufacturer) to cure the product. If you do not have the light, plan to tie this pattern on bright, sunny days. After the wing pad is finished, simply expose the fly to direct sunlight to cure it.

I'm still finding new ways to use UV Knot Sense. It's a fun product, one that I recommend you add to the list of the glue and goo you use when tying flies. The UV Knot Sense style of wing pad can also be used along with bead-chain eyes when tying any of your favorite nymph patterns.

Materials List

HOOK:	#12 or #14 regular nymph or wet-fly hook.
THREAD:	Tan or brown 6/0.
TAIL:	Pheasant-tail fibers.
EYES:	Black bead chain.
SUPERGLUE:	Used to prevent the eyes from twisting.
RIB:	Small dark brown or black vinyl ribbing.
BODY:	Brown hare's-ear dubbing.
LEGS:	Pheasant-tail fibers.
WING PAD:	UV Knot Sense (a Loon product).

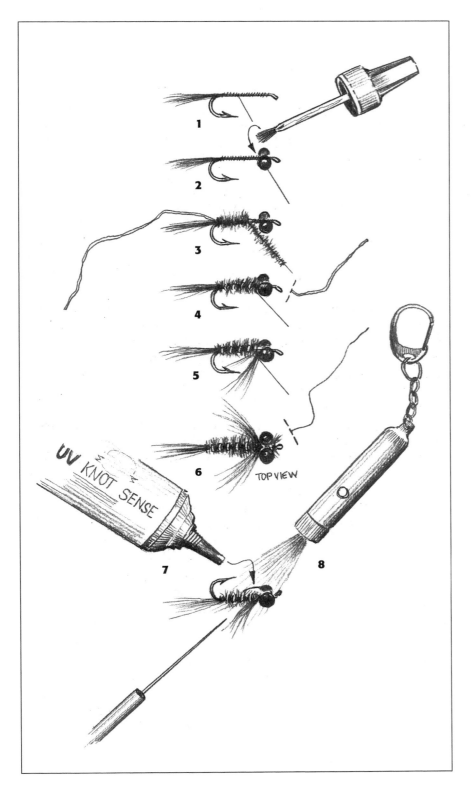

1. Attach the thread and tie on the tail.

2. Tie the bead-chain eyes in place. Apply a drop of superglue between the eyes to prevent them from twisting.

3. Attach the length of ribbing material, then start applying dubbing fur to the thread.

4. Complete the dubbing, tapering the body toward the back of the eyes. Wrap the ribbing forward to form a segmented body, tie off, and remove the excess.

5. Tie in the legs, wet-fly style, directly behind the eyes, facing out away from the body.

6. Apply a little dubbing in front and back, figure-eight between the eyes of the fly, then tie off the thread.

7. Rotate the vise, turning the hook point up, or turn the fly and reposition it in the vise. Apply a small amount of UV Knot Sense to the top of the head. Use the point of a bodkin to spread the substance over the top of the eyes and about a third of the way back over the top of the body.

8. Expose the fly to an artificial UV light or direct sunlight to cure the wing pad.

Small Fry Streamer

Fly fishers often fish a variety of tiny wets and drys, but when these same anglers turn to streamer patterns, the size drastically increases. I was no different. Until a few years ago, the smallest streamers in my box were tied on #12 long-shank hooks; others were tied on hooks as large as #4s. This selection of brightly colored attractant patterns and minnow imitations had taken many good fish, but after witnessing hundreds of tiny minnows along the edge of my favorite stretch of trout water, I decided to tie up a selection of small stuff.

I was not able to identify the species. All I knew was that their backs were a medium shade of brown and they were about 3/4 inch long. At times their slender bodies were almost invisible, their heads and eyes being the dominant features.

What I needed was a pattern with a skinny body and beady eyes. I started at the front of the tiny hook. All of the eyes that I normally use were too large and far too heavy. So I decided to stink up the room by burning a little monofilament. The first several pairs of eyes were too wide. Finally I determined that after burning the first eye, I needed to trim the line to about 1/4 inch in length in order to come up with a pair of eyes small enough for the new pattern.

The rest of the design was easy. A little soft fur became the minnow's tail. Rabbit fur handled well and would add a little action to the tiny streamer as it was retrieved through the water. Next, I attached the eyes slightly back behind the eye of the hook and applied a little superglue to prevent them from twisting. Using a bit of fine dubbing fur, I tapered the body from the base of the tail to the back of the eyes. I built up the size of the head, and then covered the area between the eyes with more of the dubbing to form the dominant head on my tiny streamer.

My first attempts fished well, but artists who tie flies can't fish a pattern for very long before trying to improve its visual quality. My later creations were tied with a tiny layer of lighter-colored fur under the tail and a little touch of red under the head. I also darkened the top of the fur body and head with a permanent marking pen. The additional effort and color probably don't matter to the trout, but they make this artist happier.

I have fished the Small Fry Streamer for several seasons with great results, especially during low-water conditions. I can never be sure whether the fish take it because it looks like the tiny minnows I happened to notice along the edge of the stream, or because they mistake it for some other form of aquatic life. But what the trout think it is isn't really important seconds after the hook is set.

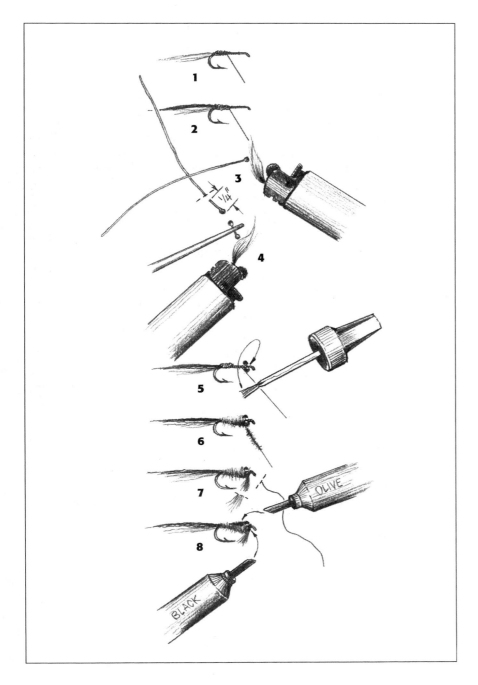

1. Attach the thread, then tie a small bunch of cream rabbit fur onto the rear of the hook. This fur should consist of more guard hairs than underfur.

2. Tie a small bunch of olive rabbit fur, mostly underfur this time, on top of the cream-colored fur.

3. Burn the end of a piece of 25- to 30-pound-test monofilament to make the first eye. Give the eye time to cool, then cut the monofilament about ¼ inch from the eye.

4. While holding the tiny piece with needlenose pliers, melt the other end of the mono to make the second eye.

5. Tie the two eyes onto the top of the hook, leaving a little room between the pair and the hook eye. Apply a drop of superglue between the eyes to prevent them from twisting.

6. Use some of the same cream rabbit fur to dub the body and the area between the eyes. It should be tapered so that the head is the widest part of this tiny minnow.

7. Tie in a few bright red hackle barbs under the eyes, then trim very short. Complete the head and tie off.

8. To finish the pattern, color the eyes with a black marker, and darken the top of the head with an olive-colored marker.

Materials List

HOOK:	#14 or #16 dry-fly hook.
THREAD:	Light brown or cream 8/0.
TAIL:	Cream rabbit fur (mostly guard hairs) with olive rabbit fur (mostly underfur) tied over the cream.
EYES:	Burned 25- to 30-pound-test monofilament.
BODY AND HEAD:	More of the same cream-colored rabbit fur (use only the underfur).
THROAT:	Six to eight bright red hackle barbs, trimmed very short.
MARKERS:	Black is used to color the eyes, and olive to darken the top of the head.
SUPERGLUE:	Used to prevent the eyes from twisting.

Floating Soft-Hackle

I have included my Epoxy Ant in my fly-tying classes for several years because it is a very easy pattern to tie, even for newcomers to the art, and the trout love it. Each time I demonstrate how to tie the foam under-body, I stop for a moment after the rear portion of the ant's body is completed and explain that other patterns might be tied with this single body segment. In the past, I attempted to create a fishable pattern with a single body segment, but somehow the pattern always evolved into a five- or six-step creation with two or three body parts.

Last winter, while reorganizing one of my wet-fly boxes, I got an idea for a different pattern. I generally fish soft-hackles, traditional wet flies, and nymphs somewhere under the surface, drifting them along at the same speed as the current, but on rare occasions I have successfully fished the wets and nymphs on top. I wondered how the fish would respond to a soft-hackle drifting along in the surface film, maybe one with a foam body.

Before the season opened, I tied up a couple dozen foam bodies and gave them a thin coat of epoxy. After the glue hardened, I painted the bodies with fingernail polish, some tan, and others a light green, brown, or black. When the paint was dry, I added a couple turns of soft-hackle to complete this simple pattern.

Field-testing my new creations was fun, since the fish were willing to participate. I believe that the floating soft-hackles are mistaken for a variety of both aquatic and terrestrial insects, making them a good choice when fishing your favorite stretch of trout water. I've done very well fishing them, especially the smaller ones with tan and light green bodies. I also like these because they are easy to see on the water.

Materials List

HOOK:	Any dry-fly hook, either standard or XL. Can be tied in a variety of sizes; I prefer #12, #14, and #16.
THREAD:	6/0 tan, brown, or black.
BODY:	Any soft high-density foam. The kickboards used by youngsters when playing in the pool are great.
HACKLE:	Soft hackle from a pheasant or partridge.
FIVE-MINUTE EPOXY:	Used to coat the foam body.
FINGERNAIL POLISH:	Used to paint the body the color of your choice.
HEAD CEMENT:	Used to complete the head.

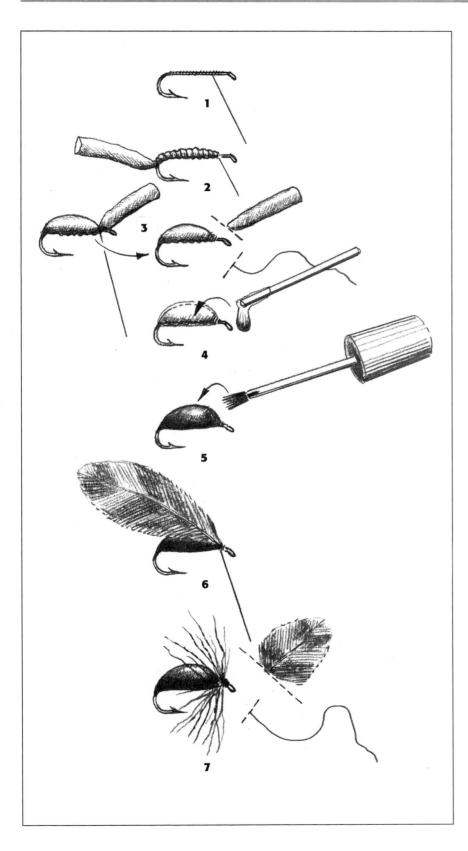

1. Attach the thread, and then wrap a base along the entire length of the hook shank.

2. Attach the foam on the top of the hook, then make enough wraps to smooth out any excess along the length of the hook. Wrap the thread back slightly beyond the bend, and then return to the front.

3. Pull the foam forward, and make several wraps of thread slightly behind the eye of the hook. Cut off the excess foam, then wrap over any remaining material at the front of the body, and tie off the thread.

4. Coat the entire body with five-minute epoxy. (Don't use too much or the pattern will not float.) Put the fly on an epoxy wheel or turn in the vise until the glue hardens.

5. After the epoxy has hardened, paint the body any color you like with fingernail polish.

6. Reattach the thread and tie in a soft hackle.

7. Wrap two or three turns of the hackle behind the eye of the hook. Remove the excess hackle, form a nicely shaped head, and tie off. A drop of head cement completes the pattern.

Easy Parachute Dry Fly

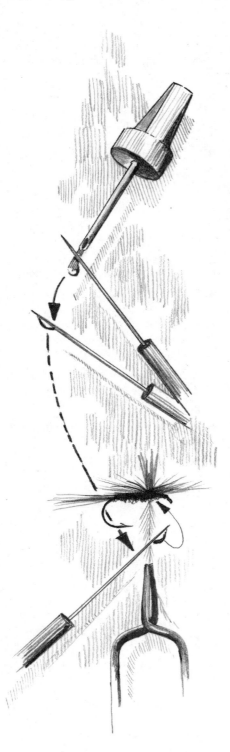

I refer to dry flies that are tied using this method as Easy Parachutes. I can't take credit for coming up with this technique. In fact, it would probably be quite a research project to find out who originally developed this method.

The Easy Parachute was passed on to me last winter at the monthly meeting of the Hudson Valley Fly Fishers. This small group of fly fishers are all very capable tiers and great friends, each willing to pass on any new tying techniques they have learned since the last meeting. Each month, one of the members is our featured instructor. This gives each of us the opportunity to teach any new methods we've learned at the vise. Bruce Corwin was our instructor last November. He had several great methods to pass on during this particular meeting, and he saved the best for last. Minutes after he showed the group the Easy Parachute, we were all searching for our supply of superglue.

The Easy Parachute method is a much easier way to tie a parachute dry fly. It is especially useful when attempting to tie very small parachutes. It is also a very durable fly. I have never had one come apart, even after being chewed on by fish.

Since the Easy Parachute is really a tying method rather than a specific pattern, the choice of materials depends on the particular dry fly you are attempting to tie. However, I would still like to make a few comments and suggestions.

Materials List

POST: I have successfully used the inter-core from large Mylar piping for posts and spent wings for many years. Some of the piping has a soft cotton core that isn't usable, but the fiber core found in most of the larger piping is very similar to Zylon. This inter-core (which is usually discarded) is a wonderful substitute for the rather expensive materials often used for posts.

BODY: I indicated a dubbed body, but this tying method works just as well with quill, floss, or other types of materials.

SUPERGLUE: The brands that come with a brush applicator are recommended. I also suggest that you use the superglue sparingly. If you use more than is necessary, your flies will turn into works of stone, rather than works of art. Transferring the superglue from the brush to your bodkin, and then to the fly will help you control the amount of glue that is finally applied to the pattern.

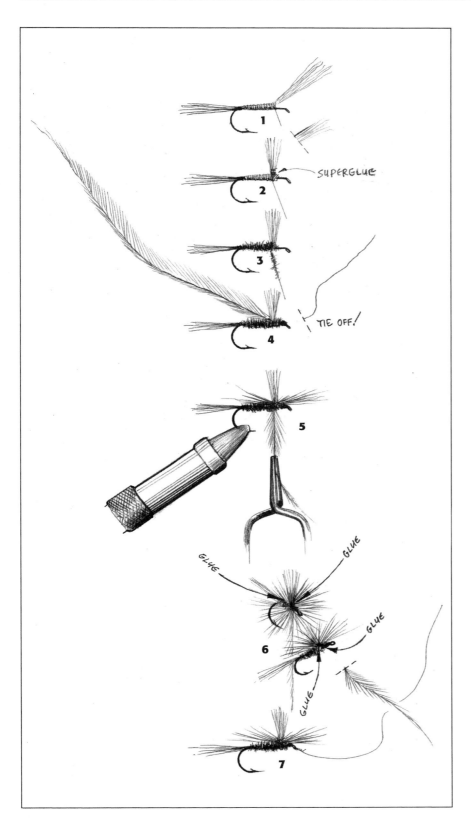

1. Attach the thread, then tie on the tail and the post.

2. Make several wraps in front of the post to support it in an upright position, and then make a couple of wraps around the base. Complete this step by trimming the post to length. A tiny amount of superglue may also be applied to the base of the post, but don't use too much, or the post will end up as hard as a rock.

3. Dub the body between the base of the tail and the rear of the post.

4. Tie in the hackle at the base of the post, and then complete the dubbing and *tie off* the head.

5. Wrap the hackle around the base of the post. Each wrap should be under the previous wraps of hackle. After completing the parachute, hang the hackle pliers behind the fly to finish this step.

6. Apply a tiny drop of superglue to the top of the hackle, close to the base of the post. Repeat on the other side. Also apply superglue under the hackle close to the body and repeat on the other side. Transferring the superglue from the bottle or brush onto the tip of a bodkin before applying makes the process easier. After the glue has dried, remove the excess hackle.

7. Shows the completed Easy Parachute Dry Fly.

Baggy Nymph

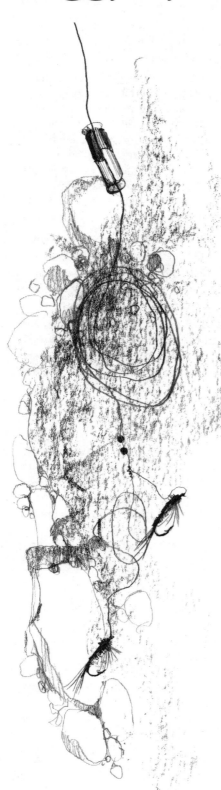

The body of this pattern is made from strips cut from a gallon size zip-lock bag. Place the bag on a piece of cardboard, and then tape it along the top and bottom. Pull the plastic tight when applying tape to the bottom. After the bag is taped securely to the cardboard, cut the plastic bag into strips using a metal straightedge and an X-acto knife. The width of the strips will vary slightly, but try to cut them between 1/8 and 3/16 of an inch wide.

I've experimented with several methods when applying color to the Baggy Nymph's body. The best-looking and most durable body was achieved using a combination of a marker and clear fingernail polish. The very top of the body is colored with the marker, and then the area is coated with the clear polish. Make sure that the polish has filled all of the spaces between the monofilament ribbing. After applying the clear polish, I wipe the sides up toward the top of the body with my finger. This removes the excess polish from the sides, keeping most of the color on top. Some of the color will remain along the ribbing, segmenting the body, and giving it a very buggy appearance.

The color can be changed with your choice of marker. I even colored a few patterns on both the top and bottom, achieving some really interesting results. Just remember to let the nail polish dry before starting the second color.

Materials List

HOOK:	#10 nymph hook.
THREAD:	Tan or brown 6/0.
TAIL:	Brown hackle barbs.
RIB:	4X tippet material.
BODY:	Strips cut from a zip-lock bag.
COLOR:	Your choice of permanent marker.
CLEAR NAIL POLISH:	Used over the marker color.
LEGS:	Soft portion from an emu feather, or your choice of hackle.
THORAX:	Any medium gray dubbing fur.
SUPERGLUE:	Used to coat top of thorax and head of the fly.

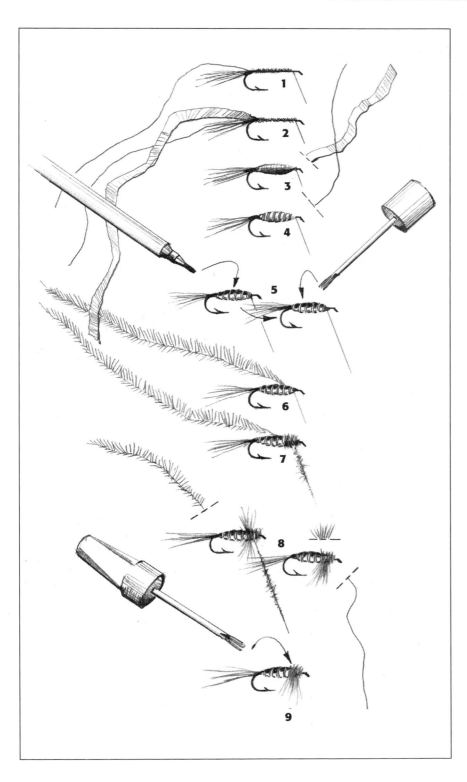

1. Attach the thread; tie in the tail and the monofilament rib.

2. Tie in the baggy strip.

3. Wrap the baggy strip to form a tapered body, then tie off the strip and remove the excess.

4. Complete the rib, tie it off and remove the excess.

5. Color the top of the body with the marker, coat with clear polish then wipe the sides.

6. Attach the emu feather.

7. Complete the dubbed thorax, stopping with the thread positioned at the back of the thorax as shown in the drawing.

8. Wrap the emu feather (two turns) around the back of the thorax, tie it off and remove the excess. Apply a tiny bit of dubbing to the thread, and then wrap through the thorax toward the head of the fly, and tie off. Remove the emu filaments from the top of the fly to complete this step.

9. Coat the top of the thorax and the head of the fly with superglue to complete the pattern.

Midnight Snack

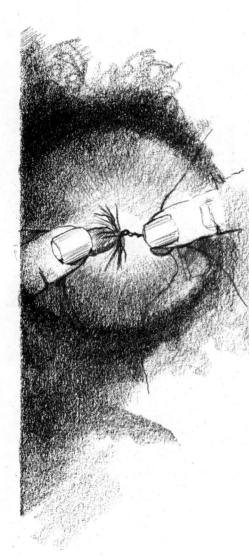

If there was a big trout under the maple, it wasn't going to be as easy to catch. If the fish saw me, it would refuse my best efforts, so I was especially careful to stay low and close to the bank. Several times the terrestrial drifted down through the run, but nothing took the offering. Determining that the tippet might be a bit heavy, I reluctantly went to 7X and put the tiny hopper back on the water.

I almost jumped out of my waders when a huge fish took the offering, but somehow I managed to set the hook. The trout leaped, then turned and headed for the far bank. I put all the pressure I dared on the fine tippet. It was not enough. Seconds after I'd hooked the fish, it reached the roots of the maple tree and broke me off.

Over the next few weeks, this same fish collected nearly a dozen of my favorite terrestrial patterns. I mentioned my experience with the large trout to my wife one evening. She just smiled and reminded me that I had not night-fished the creek this season.

That night, I walked along the edge of the field, and then turned into the tree line along the side of the stream. I missed the spot that would have positioned me below the huge maple, but I decided that fishing a couple pools would give me some practice before I attempted to present a fly to a larger quarry. The choice was a good one. I caught and released three decent fish on a moth pattern before reaching a spot downstream of the maple.

Upstream from me, the tree and the water under it appeared to be a mass of black. I knew the distance between the lower branches of the maple and the water's surface was 5 or 6 feet. An easy cast, I thought, as I pulled line from the reel and cast it forward into the darkness.

Nothing. I made another cast, attempting to put the moth a little closer to the far side of the bank. The instant the fly hit the water, I heard a splash and felt the line tighten. The rod doubled, as the fish turned and headed for the far bank and the tree roots. I pulled hard, turning the fish. Several minutes later, the battle ended in the tail of the pool.

With the fish held safely in the net, I found a place to sit along the bank. I located my small flashlight and turned it on to get a better look at my quarry. The brown was huge, but it was the color, not its size, that amazed me. As I released it back into the pool, I hoped that I would catch it again some bright, sunny day so that I might capture it on film. During the remaining weeks of the season, the fish collected a lot more of my flies, and I never got my photo.

Over the past thirty years, I have caught many big trout while night-fishing. I took them on a variety of large flies, but most of the really huge trout were caught on the moth imitations. The most productive moth flies were the lighter-colored ones, tied with white, light green, or tan materials. I find this rather interesting, since the vast majority of my other night flies are all black.

Materials List

HOOK: Mustad 9671, #8.

THREAD: White 3/0 flat waxed nylon to spin the deer hair; light gray 6/0 to complete the pattern.

BODY: Spun and trimmed deer hair, white or light gray.

WINGS AND LEGS: Blue-gray rooster pheasant feathers.

HEAD CEMENT: Used to coat the wings and finish the head.

SUPERGLUE GEL: Used to position wings over the top of the body.

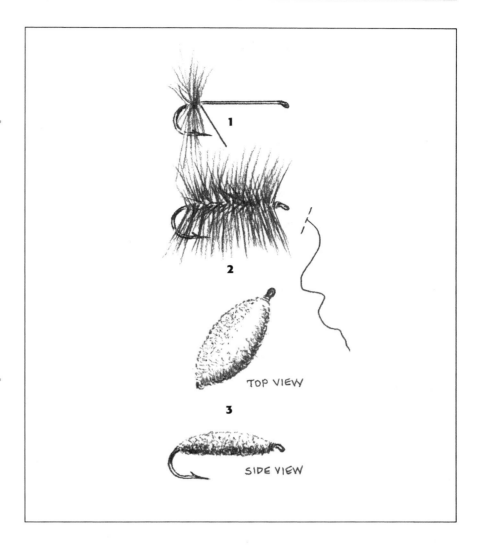

1. Attach the thread at the bend of the hook, and start spinning the deer hair.
2. Cover the entire hook shank with the spun deer hair, and tie off the thread.
3. Trim the body to the desired shape: rounded and rather flat.

4. Select two soft feathers from a pheasant skin. I prefer the blue-gray feathers found on the rear portion of the saddle.

5. Apply a generous amount of head cement to the feathers, then pull them through your fingers to work in the cement. This process will stiffen and narrow the feathers. After the glue has dried, round off the ends with scissors.

6. After reattaching the thread, apply a little superglue gel to one side of the top of the body. (The glue helps position the wings flat against the top of the body.) Tie in the first wing feather before the gel dries.

7. Apply a little more gel to the other side of the body, and tie in the second wing feather.

8. Tie in another soft pheasant hackle.

9. Make three turns of hackle, tie it off, and remove the excess. Trim the hackle from the top of the fly, form the head, and tie off the thread. A drop of head cement completes the Midnight Snack.

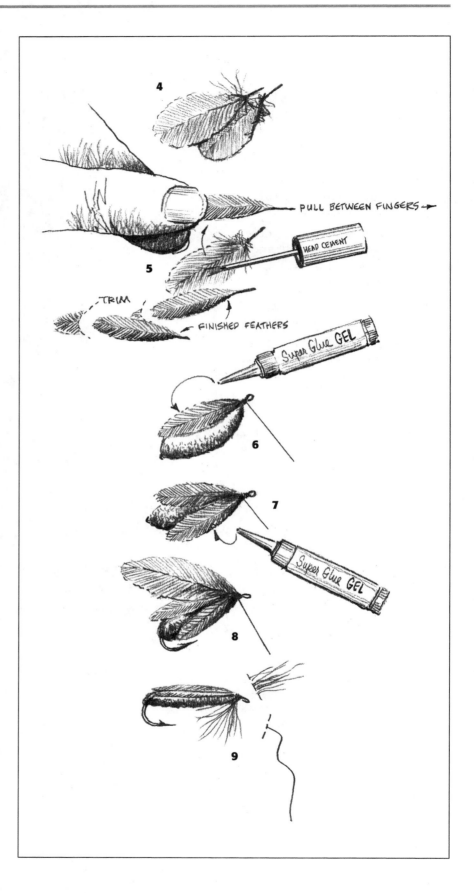

Extended-Body Dry Fly

While going through one of my fly boxes, I noticed that many of my mayfly imitations were tied with extended bodies. I have always felt that the elongated body of a mayfly was the dominant feature of the insect, and I've been willing to take the additional time required to tie these drys with their tails and fannies extending well beyond the bend of the hook.

Tying my extended-body flies generally took twice as long as a conventional dry fly. I tried several techniques and materials but wasn't able to develop a better, quicker method of building them. Eventually I decided that it was time to sit down and make a serious attempt at solving the problem.

A fly-fishing partner at a north-country lodge many years back used a different method. It was slow and messy, but it did work for larger patterns. He held the tail material against the side of the bodkin, dipped the dubbing fur into an open container of head cement, and then wrapped the dripping fur around the point of the bodkin to form the tail. After forming the body, he pulled the sticky mess off the bodkin and allowed it to dry before trimming and attaching it to the hook.

Although I wasn't crazy about this method, I had to admit that the head cement did keep the tail together, and using a bodkin or some other kind of needle seemed to work. I borrowed a needle from my wife's sewing kit and clamped it into the jaws of my vise. I then attached the tying thread, tied on three Micro Fibetts as tails, and dubbed a tapered body. After painting the body with a little head cement, I tried to slide it off the end of the needle. No good. The body came off the needle in the form of an unusable mass of sticky fur.

I tried two more times. Both attempts failed. The dubbed fur came off the needle in the form of a hollow cone, much too fragile to be used. Determining that the needle was too big, I clamped a much smaller needle in the vise, tied on the tails, and again dubbed the body. This time I didn't coat it with head cement. Instead, I gently twisted the body around the point of the needle to get it started, then carefully pulled it off. The result was a perfectly formed extended body.

After finishing several more bodies, I gave them a light coat of head cement and set them aside to dry. Once the glue had dried, I attached the bodies and performed the remaining steps required to complete the pattern. Finally I had found a quick way to make an Extended-Body Dry Fly.

Materials List

HOOK: Any dry-fly hook.

THREAD: 6/0 or 8/0, matching the color to the pattern.

TAIL, BODY, HACKLE, AND WING: These materials depend on the particular pattern you are tying.

SUPERGLUE: Used at the base of the tail to make the extended body more durable.

HEAD CEMENT: Used on the body and to finish the head.

SEWING NEEDLE: Used to support extended body and tail.

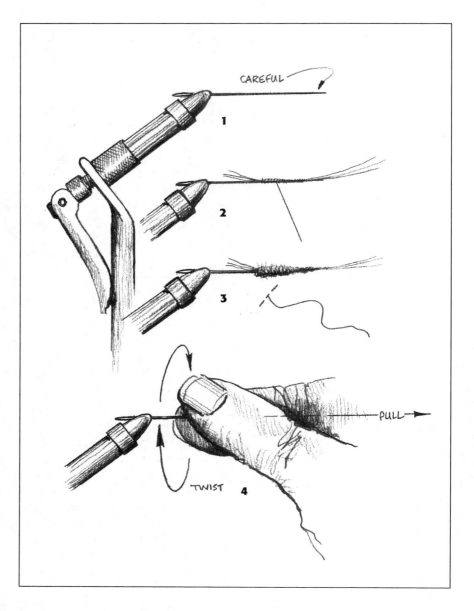

1. Clamp a small sewing needle into the jaws of the vise, with the sharp end pointing out. Be careful; I've stuck myself a couple times.

2. Attach the thread near the end of the needle. Tie in the tail, using material long enough to go all the way through the extended body.

3. Dub a tapered body on the end of the needle, and tie off the thread.

4. Gently twist the body, and then pull it off the needle.

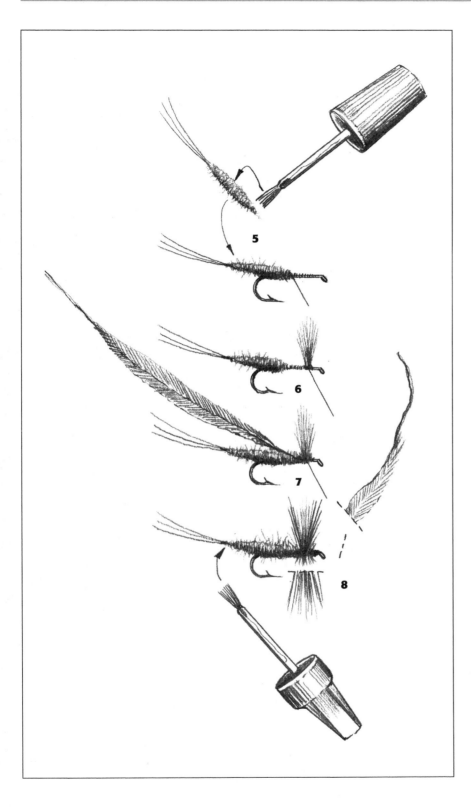

5. Apply a little head cement to the body, and set it aside to dry. After the glue has dried, tie the body onto the rear portion of the hook.

6. Tie on the wings, using whatever material and style you want.

7. Complete the body with a little more dubbing, and tie in the hackle.

8. Wind the hackle, remove the excess, and tie off the thread. Apply a drop of head cement to the head. A tiny drop of superglue at the base of the tail makes the extended body more durable. I prefer to trim off the bottom portion of the hackle, but that is entirely up to you.

Saltwater Creations

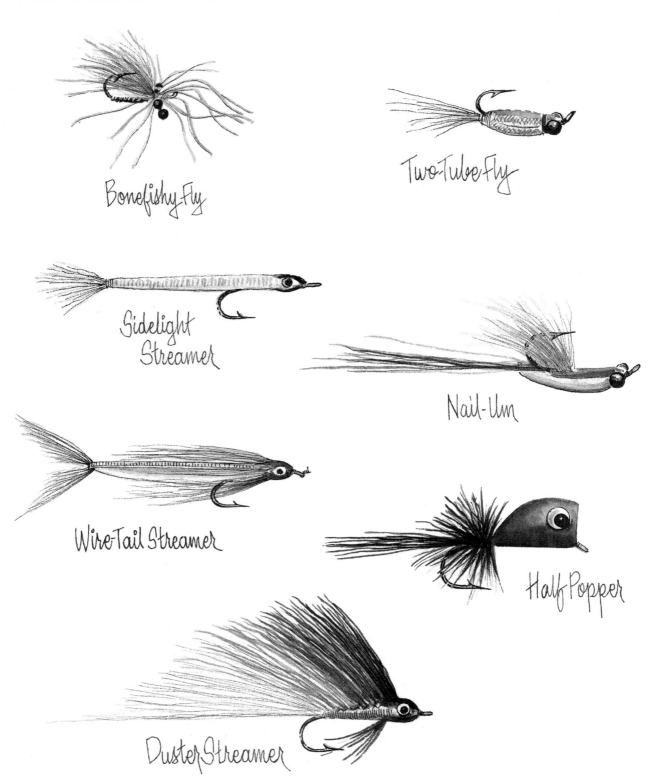

Bonefishy Fly

Two-Tube Fly

Sidelight Streamer

Nail-Um

Wire-Tail Streamer

Half Popper

Duster Streamer

Bonefishy Fly

This new bonefish fly didn't just happen. Long before the thread was attached to the hook, I'd already established what I wanted the fly to do seconds after it was wet. First off, I wanted a pattern that would land upright every time it hit the bottom. The fly also had to remain upright while it sat on the bottom. Adding a couple extra pieces of bead chain solved all of the stability issues.

The next requirement on the agenda was action. Soft fur tied over the back would add a little action to the pattern, but I wanted a fly that would come alive when it was slowly retrieved along the bottom. I envisioned a pattern that could be cast well ahead of a cruising fish, and then allowed to sink to the bottom. When a bonefish was within sight of the offering, the fly would be inched slowly forward, bringing it to life, triggering an instant response from the fish. After many failed attempts and several hours of dragging prototypes along the bottom of the test tank, I happened upon a creation that really did come to life when it was inched along.

I got the opportunity to field-test this fly during a trip to South Andros in the Bahamas. Dozens of times I cast the Bonefishy Fly ahead of a cruising fish and allowed it to sink to the bottom. As the bonefish approached the fly, I inched it forward, bringing it to life. More often than not, the fly's lifelike action resulted in a take, a hookup, and a screaming reel. I used other flies during the first couple days of the trip, but the Bonefishy Fly took more fish than any other pattern. By the third day, everyone at the lodge was successfully fishing the Bonefishy Fly.

Even if you haven't booked a trip to the bonefish flats, I strongly suggest that you tie and try a few of these flies. This design rides with the hook point up, rarely snags, and has great action when retrieved along the bottom. It is my favorite bonefish pattern, but larger Bonefishy Flies have taken a variety of both freshwater and saltwater gamefish. Try it in a variety of sizes and colors. Bonefish are only one of the species that think it looks like food.

Materials List

HOOK:	#4 or #6 stainless steel.
THREAD:	Bright pink 3/0 flat waxed nylon.
EYES:	Four pieces of black bead chain.
WING:	Cream, pink, or pinkish gray arctic fox fur.
LEGS:	Small tan Spanflex (made by Wapsi).
SUPERGLUE:	Used to prevent the eyes from twisting on hook shank.

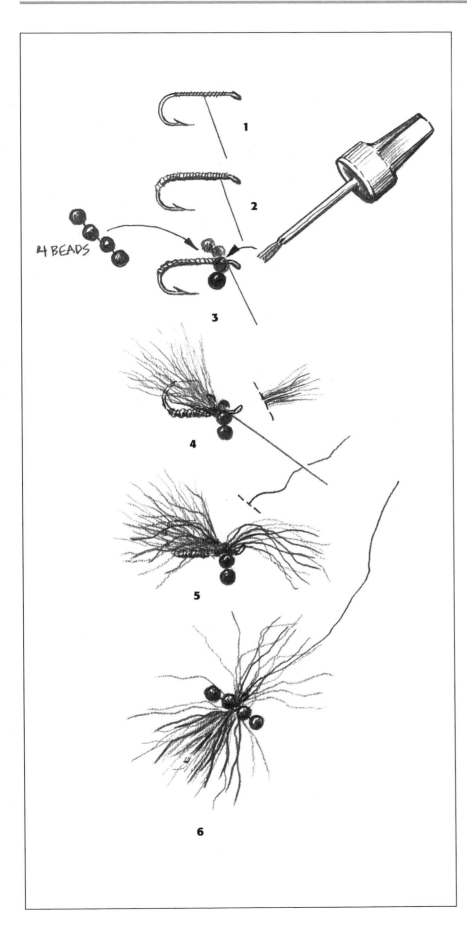

4 BEADS

1. Attach the thread to the hook shank.

2. Cover the hook shank with three or four layers of thread.

3. Tie the bead-chain eyes to the front of the hook. Leave a little room between the bead chain and the eye of the hook. After the eyes are secured, add a drop of superglue to prevent them from twisting on the hook shank.

4. Turn the fly in the vise so the hook point is up, tie in the arctic fox wing, and clip the excess fur. Remove the guard hairs. Using only the soft underfur improves the action of the wing in the water.

5. Tie about a dozen strands of the tan Spanflex on top of the hook, just in front of the bead-chain eyes. Lift the Spanflex extending in front of the fly, make a couple wraps behind the hook eye, and tie off the thread. Half of this material is left facing forward. The ends of the Spanflex touch bottom when the fly is inched forward, making the legs look as if they are actually crawling.

6. The completed Bonefishy Fly, seen from above.

Two-Tube Fly

This is an extremely versatile pattern. If the Two-Tube Fly is tied on a hook that has a standard-length shank, the end product will have a wider silhouette. Use the same piping on a hook with an extended shank, and the fly becomes long and slender, more minnowlike. Tie it on a #6 or #8 hook, and it may be presented to everything from bluegills to bonefish. Increase the hook size slightly, and it may take a stream smallmouth or a large brown trout. Increase the size of the hook and the piping, and the Two-Tube is a good choice when the stripers or bluefish are busting bait. By changing the type and size of the hook and the color and size of the piping, you can produce a wide variety of flies for both fresh- and saltwater pursuits.

The Two-Tube can be tied to swim just under the surface or drop like a stone into deeper water. By using different eyes, similar-looking patterns can be fished anywhere within the water column. Tie it with lead dumbbell eyes and it sinks like a stone. Bead-chain eyes will also turn the fly over (hook point up), but the sink rate is slower. Plastic eyes will cause the fly to sink very slowly and swim with the hook point down. It is important to remember which way a particular Two-Tube will swim before applying a little color to the "back" of a finished fly.

Materials List

HOOK: Choose a hook for either fresh or salt water, in a size appropriate for the fly you are tying.

THREAD: White 3/0 flat waxed nylon to attach the piping; red 6/0 behind the eyes.

MYLAR PIPING: Experiment with different sizes and colors.

EYES: Plastic, bead-chain, or lead dumbbell eyes may be used, depending on the sink rate desired.

SUPERGLUE: Used to prevent the eyes from twisting.

HEAD CEMENT: Used to coat the base of the tail, the red thread, and the head.

WATERPROOF MARKER: Used to add a little color and detail.

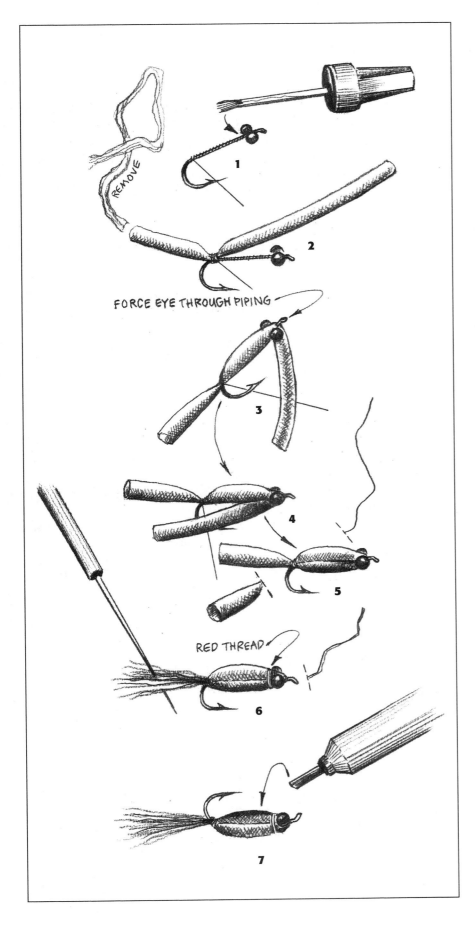

FORCE EYE THROUGH PIPING

RED THREAD

1. Attach the thread, tie in the eyes, and then return the thread to the rear portion of the hook. Add a drop of superglue between the eyes to prevent twisting.

2. Pull the core out of a piece of piping about two and a half times the length of the hook, and attach the piping to the rear of the hook.

3. Center the piping in front of and between the eyes, then force the eye end of the hook through the piping.

4. Pull the piping back under the hook shank.

5. Secure the piping to the rear of the hook, remove the excess, and tie off the thread. Squeeze the sides of the piping to improve the shape of the fly.

6. Fray the tail with a bodkin, then attach the red thread just behind the eyes. Make five or six wraps and tie off. Use head cement to coat the thread at the rear of the hook, the red thread, and the head of the fly.

7. A waterproof marker may be used to color the back of the Two-Tube, keeping in mind whether the fly will swim with the hook point up or down.

Side/Lights Streamer

Years back, Massachusetts fly fishermen Richard Murphy and Mike Martinek discovered a great new ribbon and developed several very productive saltwater streamers using this material. Mike gave me a sample of the ribbon at a fly-tying show, suggesting that I give it a try. Receiving a pack of a new tying material normally sends me running for the vise, but my inventory of new materials had been piling up. Finally, after nearly a year, I got the chance to sit down at the vise and experiment with this new ribbon.

The ribbon, called Side/Lights Body Scale, looked great, having the flash and the transparent quality of many baitfish found in both fresh and salt water. The ribbon was also very user-friendly, as I folded, cut, and tied some onto a small hook. After attaching the ribbon, I tied a little bright red hackle under the head, then a few strands of fine FisHair over the top. I tied several more prototypes using a variety of materials, then stuck on some eyes, coated the heads with thirty-minute epoxy, and put them on the wheel. As I sat watching them turn, I suddenly determined that they were all much too complicated.

Starting over, I simply folded the length of ribbon and wound a few wraps of thread around the end to form the tail. Then I attached the ribbon to the front of the hook and tied off the thread. I positioned a pair of stick-on eyes on either side of the head, coated the head of the small streamer with epoxy, and put it on the wheel. After it had hardened, I used a fine red marker to indicate the gills and painted the top of the head with a little silver fingernail polish. This small, simple Side/Lights Streamer looked as if it had just jumped out of a minnow bucket.

The Side/Lights Streamer is a very productive, easy-to-tie pattern that will catch a wide variety of both fresh- and saltwater species, but it is especially effective when fly fishing for albacore. When these fish are keyed in on small bait, this pattern has proven to be the best albacore fly I've tied onto the end of a tippet. Tie it and try it.

Materials List

HOOK:	Choose one suitable for the size of streamer you are tying.
THREAD:	White 3/0 flat waxed nylon.
BODY:	1/4- or 3/8-inch silver or gold Side/Lights Body Scale. (Many different craft store ribbons may be used when tying this creation.)
EYES:	Stick-ons or painted.
COLOR:	Your choice of nail polish, paints, or markers.
GLUES:	Head cement, thirty-minute epoxy, superglue, and Zip Kicker.

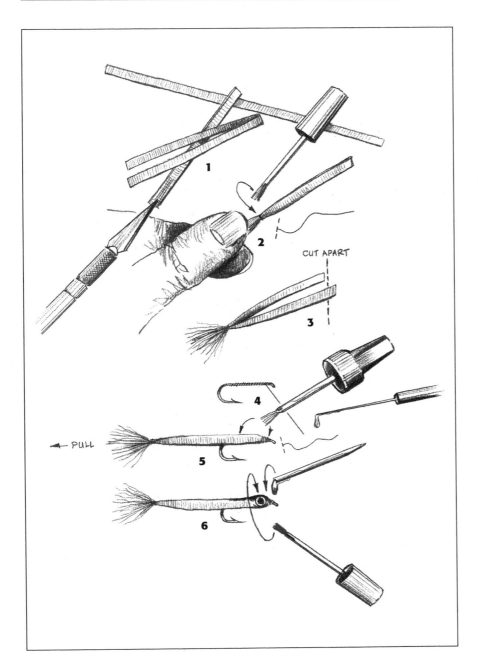

1. Cut the ribbon to the desired length. Fold the piece in half, then make several lengthwise cuts through the ends to form the tail.

2. Tie off the base of the tail with a length of 3/0 tying thread. Remove the excess thread, and finish with a drop of head cement.

3. This is what the ribbon looks like before it is attached to the hook.

4. Attach the thread, then cover the straight portion of the hook shank with thread.

5. Position the ribbon on either side of the hook, tie it in place, finish off the head, and tie off the thread. Apply a few drops of superglue to the ribbon, but not beyond the bend of the hook. Pull the ribbon tight as the superglue is drying. (Zip Kicker may be used to hurry up the drying time.) This results in a nice, straight streamer.

6. Position a pair of stick-on eyes on either side of the head. Coat the head with thirty-minute epoxy, and put the streamer on the wheel to harden. Add a little color after the epoxy has cured. A variety of Side/Lights Streamers may be made using this simple tying method.

Nail-Um

Over the past ten years, many of my better patterns have evolved from something purchased from one of the local craft stores, but recently I found another marvelous source of strange fly-tying stuff: The dollar stores often stock items that can be put to good use by the innovative tier. Recently I found a real bargain: I was able to buy more than seven hundred fake fingernails for less than $5. Yes, I know this is a rather bizarre item, but I liked the shape and thought I could come up with an interesting pattern using the strange pieces of plastic.

I spent the next few weeks experimenting with the fake fingernails, rejecting a handful of prototypes. Finally I came up with a combination of materials and technique that seemed to work. In fact, I thought the new creation looked pretty good. I tied dozens of Nail-Ums at the shows. I've even included the pattern in one of my fly-tying classes. Many of my fellow tiers kidded me about my choice of materials, but they also liked the looks of my new creation.

Everyone seemed to like the fly, but the real test was how it would do on the water: How would it look, how would it fish, and what would the fish think of it? I also wondered how durable it would be if a fish actually decided to eat this foolish pattern. It passed with high marks. The Nail-Um didn't cast any differently than any other weighted fly, and the action in the water was great, but most important, the fish loved it. It was also more durable than I had even hoped. I surely didn't want to break a nail every time I caught a fish!

I don't ever want to be thought of as an authority on fake fingernails, but I do feel that some are better than others. Though they can be painted any color using your favorite fingernail polish, those that are left unpainted have a very interesting quality that makes them a much better choice. They are semitransparent, and when the colors of the tail and body are seen from underneath, the pattern resembles a shrimp. Consequently, the Nail-Um is great when fishing waters containing this particular food source.

I have had the best results when the materials were a mixture of pink, orange, and reddish orange, but you should experiment with other color combinations when tying these unique flies.

Materials List

HOOK:	Choose one with a shank about three-quarters the length of the fingernail.
THREAD:	White 3/0 flat waxed nylon thread.
EYES:	Bead chain.
TAIL:	Any natural or synthetic material, preferably pink or pale orange.
BODY:	Bright pink arctic fox. (I use this material in many of my patterns because it has great action in the water and is very durable.)
UNDERBODY:	Fake fingernail. (The dollar stores are a great source for this material.)

(continued on next page)

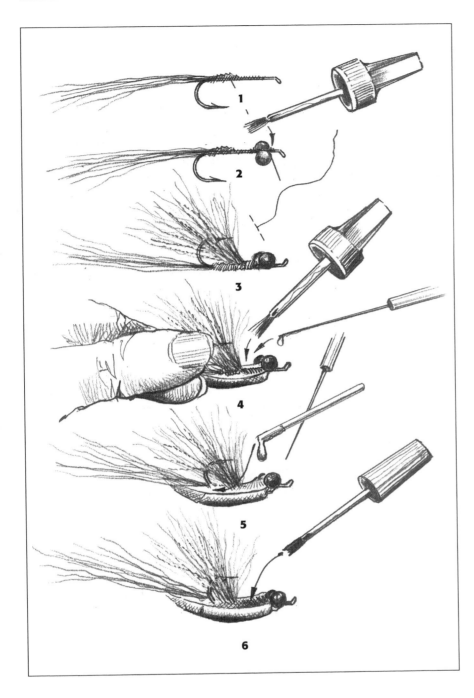

1. Attach the thread and tie in the tail.

2. Attach a pair of bead-chain eyes just behind the eye of the hook. Apply a little superglue between the eyes and along the hook shank to prevent twisting.

3. Rotate the fly in the vise, then attach the arctic fox fur body at the midway point of the hook shank. Tie in five or six strands of orange Krystal Flash, and tie off the fly.

4. Position the hook along the center of the fingernail, with the back of the eyes against the front edge of the nail. Apply a generous amount of superglue along the hook shank just behind the eyes. Check the position of the hook. When everything is lined up properly, apply a drop of Zip Kicker to instantly harden the superglue. This is a quick, easy way to position the hook in the nail. It works better than trying to keep everything lined up while the epoxy hardens.

5. Fill the inside of the fingernail with five-minute epoxy. Use your bodkin to work some of the epoxy back along both sides of the hook shank; doing so results in a better-looking, stronger body.

6. Paint over the top of the epoxy with pink fingernail polish to complete the pattern.

Materials List (continued)

KRYSTAL FLASH: Five or six strands of orange to add a little flash to the pattern.

SUPERGLUE: Used to prevent the eyes from twisting and position the hook inside the fingernail.

ZIP KICKER: Used to harden the superglue once the hook is in the proper position.

FIVE-MINUTE EPOXY: Used to fill the inside of the body.

FINGERNAIL POLISH: Pink polish is painted over the epoxy to hide any yellowing, thus preserving the future visual quality of the fly.

Wire-Tail Streamer

I suggested several patterns and got a response from my guide similar to a pitcher waving off signs from the catcher. Finally he recommended a shiny fly, approving the third fly I removed from my box and held up for inspection. I tied the Silversides Streamer onto the end of the leader and dropped it on the water in front of the boat. On the second strip, a fish hammered it. That was the way it was all morning. The guide was absolutely right. The specks wanted shiny flies.

By the end of the second morning, my inventory of shiny streamers was down to a precious few. After lunch, I sat down at the vise to replenish my supply. Everything was going great until I realized that my tying stuff did not include a roll of the shiny ribbon used for the body on the Silversides Streamer.

I found another roll of ribbon in the bottom of the box. It was different, but it was shiny. As I started to shape the body, I noticed that a wire ran along both edges of the ribbon. I folded the ribbon and cut out the body so that the wire ran along the top, figuring that the wire would make the streamer more durable.

To keep the ends of the tail together, I folded and cut the ribbon so that the bend in the wire was at the end of the body. After attaching the body to the hook, I sat there trying to decide whether the new ribbon was an adequate substitute. Then I just happened to push the point of my scissors down in between the fold at the end of the tail. When I removed the scissors, there was a gap in the ribbon. I prepared a small bundle of synthetic fiber and inserted it in the loop in the end of the tail, then pulled the material back with my fingers, forming a V shape.

The instant I pulled the material back, I knew what to do to complete the tail. I used superglue at the base and added a drop of Zip Kicker to hurry up the drying process. A little trimming was all that was needed to complete a very realistic tail. I had tried to tie realistic-looking tails on my streamers for years, and though some looked great, those earlier attempts often took longer than tying the rest of the streamer. The method used for the Wire-Tail Streamer is quick and easy.

Materials List

HOOK:	Any saltwater hook that will accommodate the streamer you are tying.
THREAD:	White 3/0 flat waxed nylon.
BODY:	Silver ribbon 1 inch or wider. Any metallic-looking ribbon may be used, as long as it is the *wired* type. The wire is necessary to support the tail material while tying the pattern and also makes the streamer much more durable.
TAIL:	Silver Polarflash.
SUPERGLUE:	Used to secure the tail.
ZIP KICKER:	Used to instantly dry the superglue when constructing the tail.
EYES, WING, BELLY, AND HEAD:	Your choice of materials. Tying the tail was my idea. The rest of the pattern can be finished any way you see fit.

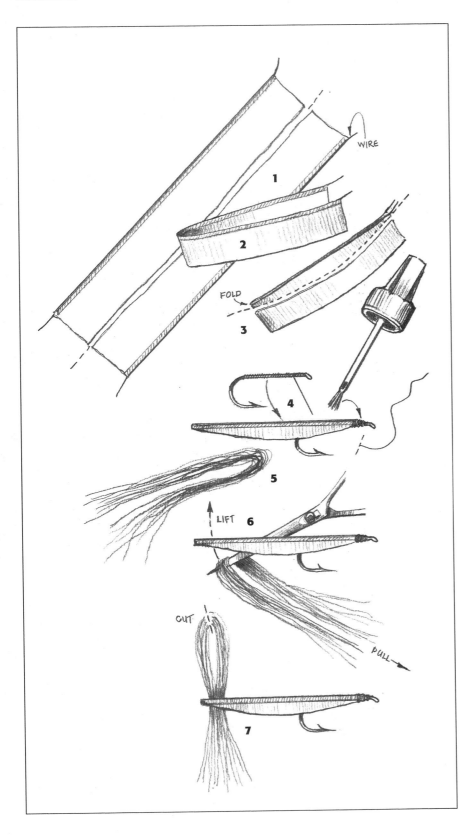

1. Cut the ribbon in half lengthwise (between the wires).

2. Fold the ribbon in half crosswise.

3. Line the wire edges together, and trim the body to shape.

4. Prewrap the hook shank with thread. Position the front of the body on either side of the hook, and secure just behind the eye. Tie off the thread and add a drop of superglue to prevent twisting.

5. Fold twenty to twenty-five strands of Polarflash (4 to 5 inches long) in half, forming a loop in the material.

6. Slide your scissors down in-between the body, and then insert the point through the loop in the Polarflash. Lift the Polarflash up through the body while lightly pulling the material back to maintain tension.

7. Adjust the tail material so that there is an equal amount on either side of the ribbon, and cut through the Polarflash at the loop.

8. Open the superglue and the Zip Kicker so that they're both ready for use. Pull the Polarflash back with your fingers, and apply a couple drops of superglue at the base of the tail on both sides of the ribbon. Use a drop of the Zip Kicker to instantly dry the superglue.

9. Trim the tail to the desired shape.

10. Tie small bunches of your favorite natural or synthetic hair over the back and underbelly of the streamer to create the shape of the body. A couple eyes of your choice and a little epoxy finish the head, completing the pattern.

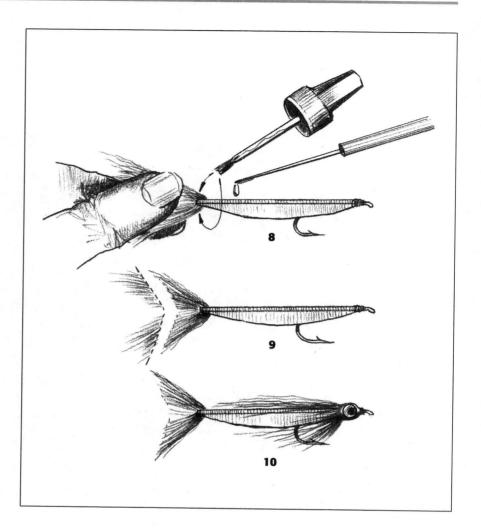

Half Popper

Years back, while making up a dozen rather large bluefish poppers, I decided to give the painted hard-foam bodies a thin coat of epoxy. I knew that doing so would add a little weight, making the poppers more difficult to cast, but I was willing to put up with this if the tough coating enabled me to catch a few more toothy critters before the popper was trashed.

I had a little epoxy left over after completing the bluefish poppers. Rather than waste it, I decided to take a quick look at some of the well-used poppers in one of my freshwater boxes. Several of the bass poppers were showing signs of hard use; giving their heads a fresh coat of epoxy might just prolong their life on the water.

Later that same week, I was casting poppers into bassy-looking cover from a canoe on my favorite pond. After an hour of beating the water, I had not triggered a single strike. I changed flies, trying different colors, sizes, and types. No takers. Finally I tied on one of the old poppers that I had recently coated with epoxy and dropped it onto the water alongside the canoe. All of the other poppers I had presented to the bass were lighter and rode much higher in the water. This popper stayed on top, but with about half of the body in the water.

It took a bit more effort to get the epoxy-coated creation into the air, but after several backcasts, I adjusted for the additional weight and dropped the offering just off the edge of the weed line. A couple casts later, I took my first bass of the afternoon. After an hour, I had caught four more, including one that might have been the mother of the first fish.

Down through the years, I have experimented with many new popper designs. The most successful creations have always been the ones that ride a little deeper in the water. Smaller, heavier poppers were fishable, but when the size of the heads was increased to something suitable for larger saltwater species, the greater weight and wind resistance really made them a pain to cast.

I make many of my popper heads out of fishing floats. While purchasing a new supply, I included some larger floats made by Comal Tackle. They were nearly 2 inches long and over 1 inch in diameter. I cut one in half, the way I normally do when turning floats into popper heads, but it didn't sit well on the 4/0 hook. I trimmed a little off the bottom, but it still didn't work. I cut another float in half, then cut one of the pieces in half again lengthwise. It seemed to work just fine, so I made up a dozen, coating six of them with epoxy.

I did not realize it at the time, but I had solved my big popper problem. As soon as I put one of the epoxy-coated Half Poppers into the air, I was amazed at how well it handled. Sure, it still felt like a large fly, but considering its size, weight, and wind resistance, this popper was a great improvement over earlier designs. Like all of the epoxy-coated creations, it pushed water when stripped, triggering frequent strikes.

Materials List

HOOK: Match to the size of the popper head. I use stainless steel hooks on all my large poppers so that they can be fished in both fresh and salt water.

THREAD: White 3/0 flat waxed nylon.

POPPER HEAD: The bright red Comal Tackle floats are my favorite for this pattern, but other floats may be used.

FINGERNAIL POLISH: White is used to paint the bottom of the head.

THIRTY-MINUTE EPOXY: Used to coat the body. If you do not have a wheel available, use five-minute epoxy and turn the popper in the vise.

FIVE-MINUTE EPOXY: Used to secure popper head to hook.

EYES: Round plastic doll eyes.

1. This float will make four Half Poppers.

2. Cut the float in half.

3. Cut each piece in half again lengthwise. Smooth any rough surfaces with fine sandpaper.

4. Cover the hook shank with thread and tie off, then secure the popper head to the hook with a little five-minute epoxy.

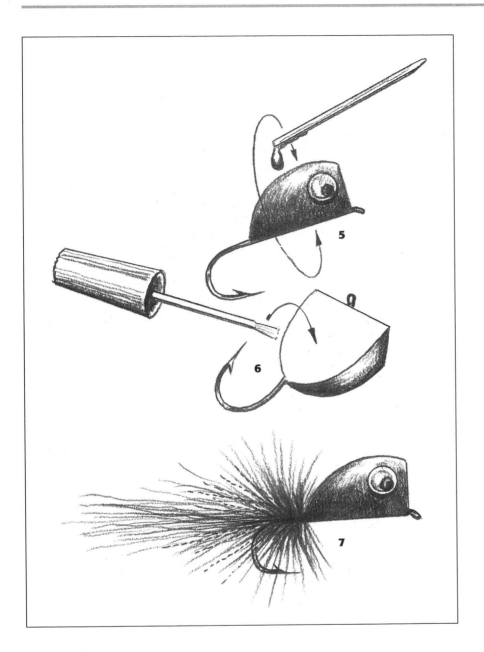

5. Coat the entire head with thirty-minute epoxy, and put the popper on an epoxy wheel to harden. After the epoxy has started to harden slightly, you can add a pair of plastic doll eyes.

6. Paint the bottom of the popper head with white fingernail polish.

7. Complete the tail. I suggest using something flashy, but any natural or synthetic material will do the job.

Duster Streamer

L ow price doesn't always mean poor quality. Several weeks back, I received a sample of a new fly-tying fiber. This new, rather pricey stuff was advertised as a wonderful addition to the tier's inventory of materials. It looked great, so I decided to put it to the test. I tied a dozen different creations using the new product but finally decided that it wasn't very tier-friendly.

That same week, I found another product that looked rather promising at a dollar store, an ordinary house duster. I purchased five different colors of dusters for less than the advertised price of one package of the other stuff. Then I sat down at the vise to give the duster fiber an honest try. This new material was great. I used it for a variety of saltwater creations, even a shrimp pattern, and found the brightly colored dusters to be a welcome addition to my ever-growing inventory of strange tying stuff.

The streamers that I created from the dusters were easy to tie, and they looked and fished great. So I will introduce you to one more strange but useful fly-tying material. Have fun experimenting with this new stuff. Duster Streamers may be tied for a variety of species simply by varying the hook size and material colors.

Materials List

HOOK:	Match to the type and size of the streamer you are tying.
THREAD:	White 3/0 flat waxed nylon.
WING:	Fibers from white, green, and blue dusters from the local dollar store were used to construct the entire fly.
EYES:	Round doll eyes.
THROAT:	Bright red fibers from duster.
FIVE-MINUTE EPOXY:	Used to attach the eyes and coat the head.
FINGERNAIL POLISH:	Used on the top and bottom of the head.

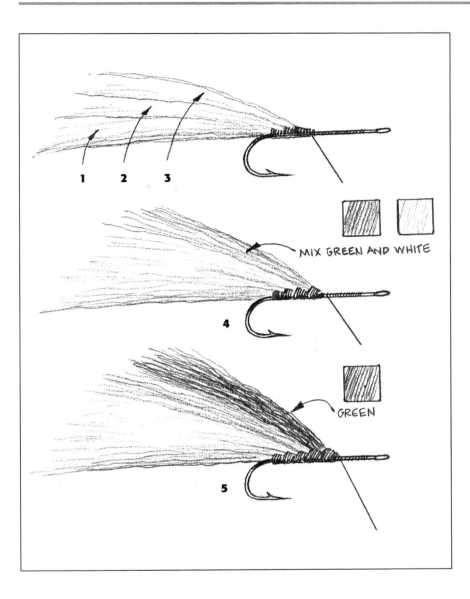

MIX GREEN AND WHITE

GREEN

1. Tie three small bundles of white duster fibers onto the rear of the hook.

2. Work the fibers between your fingers to vary the lengths of the tips, then trim the other end and attach each bundle to the hook.

3. Starting at the bend of the hook, work your way along the shank, tying each bundle slightly forward of the one before it.

4. Mix slightly smaller bundles of the green and white fibers, keeping the fibers lined up as you blend the colors together. Remove any fibers that aren't lined up properly, then trim the end of the bundle and tie it onto the hook, again slightly forward of the last bundle.

5. Prepare a bundle of the green fibers and tie it onto the hook shank slightly forward of the last one.

6. Mix smaller bundles of the blue and green fibers, removing any fibers that aren't lined up. Trim the end of the bundle, and tie it onto the hook slightly forward of the previous one.

7. Prepare a bundle of the blue fibers, and tie it onto the hook shank. Tie a small amount of the red fibers under the body of the fly to complete the tying portion of the Duster Streamer.

8. Coat the head with a little five-minute epoxy, and turn until the glue begins to thicken. Then place the eyes upside down on your tying bench. Remove the streamer from the vise, and pick up the eyes by touching them with the head. As the epoxy hardens, position the eyes to keep them lined up on either side of the head. After the first coat of epoxy has hardened, apply a second coat over the head and eyes, and turn until hardened. Paint the area between the eyes (top and bottom) with fingernail polish to match the colors of the duster fibers on the top and bottom of the fly closest to the head.

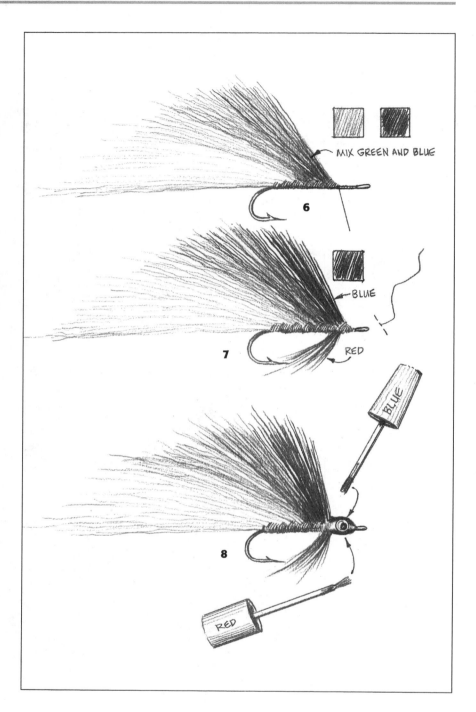

Fly-Tying Materials: Tips and Suggestions

DOUBLE LIP

BRUSH-ON

INSTANT KRAZY GLUE BRUSH-ON

bump chenille. The BC Shiner is a marvelous pattern when fishing in and around heavy cover, but the stiffer kind of chenille can be difficult to find. A bump chenille made from a softer material is often available at the local craft stores, but it is not stiff enough to make the fly weedless. The only supply of the stiffer material that I can find is packages of assorted, brightly colored bump chenille. I've used some of these brighter colors, and even though the flies look a little strange, they fish just fine.

dry cleaner bag. This thin plastic is the best choice for tying the Itsy Bitsy Spider. I've tried other thin plastics, but they did not work as well. The thin plastic from dry cleaner bags is very tier-friendly and more resistant to tearing, making the spider more durable when it is fished.

fake fingernails. I am sure that there is a limit to my choice of materials when designing patterns for magazine articles, but I was able to sneak the Nail-Um into this book. I am thrilled to pass this pattern on to you, since it is very productive on the water. Smaller ones take bonefish, but I have taken more than a dozen other saltwater species on this style of fly. Consequently, I tie dozens of Nail-Ums in a variety of sizes and colors. Fake fingernails are expensive if you purchase them from the cosmetic counter, but you can often find them in dollar stores for much less.

foam blocks. Several seasons back, a friend introduced me to Wapsi's foam blocks. He liked the foam and wanted me to try it. Since trying this particular foam, I have used it exclusively for all of my small hopper patterns. It floats forever and is very durable, even when used on terrestrials as small as size 18s. This product comes in many usable colors, but my favorite is the chartreuse because the fish love it and I can see it on the water.

knitting yarns. I mentioned two products by name for tying the Floss Fly, but hundreds of wonderful yarns are available. The yarn section of our local craft store has become a great source of fly-tying material. Shop the yarn department, and have fun experimenting with this wonderful supply of tying stuff.

mini duster. Each duster has a generous supply of soft, usable fibers. The fibers are tier-friendly and very durable. I use the duster fibers on many of my streamer patterns. This product is frequently found in the dollar stores and is available in a wide variety of colors.

mylar piping. Any color or size of Mylar piping may be used for the Two-Tube Fly. I tie and fish many variations of this pattern in both fresh and salt water. Consequently, I have accumulated quite a selection of the piping. Some of the piping has a soft, stringlike core that I simply remove and throw away, but others have cores that are very similar to Z-Lon. I use such cores for posts and spent wings on many of my dry-fly patterns.

Side/Lights ribbon. The Side/Lights ribbon recommended for the fly isn't the only kind that can be used for the Side/Lights Streamer. I have found similar products in the section displaying ribbons intended for weddings. A common one is called Modern Romance, but there are several others that work just fine for these small streamers.

superglue. Since I found superglue in a bottle with a brush applicator, I haven't used as much head cement. The tiny vials of superglue always dried up soon after they were opened. They were costly and messy. This bottle has a double rim so the lid is easily removed even after the glue hasn't been used for weeks, and the brush applicator is just wonderful when you are attempting to apply glue to a fly. Try CVS pharmacy or a craft store. When the bottle gets low, refill it with any brand of superglue purchased from a dollar store.

UV Knot Sense. This Loon product is used for the wing pad on my UV Nymph, but it can also be used to coat the bodies on many of the smaller terrestrials. I frequently use it on my UV Ants and Floating Soft-Hackles. It is available at most fly shops, since it is generally used to coat connections between backing, fly line, and leaders. It also repairs small tears in waders in just a few seconds.

wired ribbons. The Wire-Tail Streamer is an easy pattern to tie if you are using the proper ribbon. Almost any craft-store ribbon that has a strand of fine wire running along each outside edge can be used. Select a ribbon that tends not to fray after it is trimmed to shape. The foil ribbons are best when you can find them, since they do not fray when cut. The ribbon should be at least 1 inch wide.

Zip Kicker. This product is an accelerator for superglue. I frequently use it when I want to hurry up the drying process or when joining one item to another. I hold the two pieces together, apply a few drops of superglue, fiddle with the pieces until they are exactly where I want them, and then add a drop of Zip Kicker. This product comes with an atomizer top: *Don't Use It!* Spraying the Zip Kicker is messy, smelly, and uses ten times more than is really needed. I dip my bodkin into the fluid and apply a drop or two. The Zip Kicker lasts far longer with this method.

About the Author

Jay "Fishy" Fullum has been teaching fly tying classes to kids and adults for well over thirty years. His first piece of advice is that fly tying and fly fishing should always be fun. He has taken this message across the country, conducting tying and fishing seminars from Florida to Alaska.

With nearly fifteen years of commercial fly tying experience, Fishy has written articles for most of the major fly-fishing magazines. He currently serves as a columnist for *Fly Tyer* magazine and as field editor for *Fly Fishing New England.*

A retired designer and graphic artist, Fishy continues to create illustrations and watercolors to accompany his original fly designs. *Fishy's Favorites for Bass, Trout, and Salt Water* is his second book, following the popular *Fishy's Flies* (Stackpole Books 2002).

Fishy is an avid angler; with his wife and favorite fly-fishing partner, Carol, he catches everything from bluegills to bonefish. He lives in Ravena, New York.

Jay "Fishy" Fullum

Fly-Tying Classes

Fishy Fullum offers a variety of fly-tying classes on warmwater, coldwater, and saltwater patterns. Your chapter or club may also request specific Fishy flies that you wish to cover in a session. Students are asked to bring a vise, tying tools, and a selection of thread. Fishy supplies all the other materials used in class.

PowerPoint Presentations

Fishy's presentations are primarily on fly tying, and he also includes information on where and how to fish the patterns featured. Programs on warmwater, coldwater, and saltwater flies are available, and Fishy also offers a program that covers all three categories. If your chapter or club is interested in a particular type of fishing, Fishy can customize the presentation to meet your specific needs.

You might want to do a class in the morning, a fly-tying round table in the afternoon, and a PowerPoint presentation that evening. Fishy charges by the day, and not for each program. Most organizations charge a fee for the classes or other events to cover expenses. Fishy also donates items to the chapter or club which can be auctioned off at a later date.

If you are interested in a presentation, contact Fishy at fishy@mhonline.net.